CONCILIUM

THEOLOGY IN THE AGE OF RENEWAL

International Publishers of CONCILIUM

ENGLISH EDITION
Paulist Press
Glen Rock, N. J., U.S.A.

Burns & Oates Ltd.
25 Ashley Place
London, S.W.1

DUTCH EDITION
Uitgeverij Paul Brand, N.V.
Hilversum, Netherlands

FRENCH EDITION
Maison Mame
Tours/Paris, France

GERMAN EDITION
Verlagsanstalt Benziger & Co., A.G.
Einsiedeln, Switzerland

Matthias Grunewald-Verlag
Mainz, W. Germany

SPANISH EDITION
Ediciones Guadarrama
Madrid, Spain

PORTUGUESE EDITION
Livraria Morais Editora, Ltda.
Lisbon, Portugal

PASTORAL THEOLOGY

THE PASTORAL MISSION OF THE CHURCH

Vol. 3

CONCILIUM
theology in the age of renewal

PAULIST PRESS/GLEN ROCK, NEW JERSEY

NIHIL OBSTAT: Edward J. Montano, S.T.D.
Censor Librorum

IMPRIMATUR: ✠ Francis Cardinal Spellman
Archbishop of New York

February 25, 1965

The Nihil Obstat and Imprimatur are official declarations that a book or pamphlet is free of doctrinal or moral error. No implication is contained therein that those who have granted the Nihil Obstat and Imprimatur agree with the contents, opinions or statements expressed.

Library of Congress Catalogue Card Number: 65-19634

Suggested Decimal Classification: 250

BOOK DESIGN: Claude Ponsot

PAULIST PRESS
EXECUTIVE OFFICES: 21 Harristown Road, Glen Rock, New Jersey
Executive Publisher: John A. Carr, C.S.P.
Executive Manager: Alvin A. Illig, C.S.P.
Asst. Executive Manager: Thomas E. Comber, C.S.P.

EDITORIAL OFFICES: 304 W. 58th Street, New York, N.Y.
Editor: Kevin A. Lynch, C.S.P.
Managing Editor: Urban P. Intondi

Manufactured in the United States of America

CONTENTS

PART II

BIBLIOGRAPHICAL SURVEY

PART III

DO-C: DOCUMENTATION CONCILIUM

PART IV

CHRONICLE OF THE LIVING CHURCH

PREFACE

Karl Rahner, S.J./*Munich, W. Germany*
Heinz Schuster/*Saarbrücken, W. Germany*

Since the function of theology in the Church is to lay down the basis of the Church's self-awareness in a scientific manner, it cannot limit itself to the unfolding of permanent factors in the history of the Church. The present and the future of the Church, too, fall necessarily within the scope of theological thought. Only *pastoral* theology can undertake this task. But it can only do so if we no longer leave it to collect and transmit norms, regulations and pastoral experiences for use by the clergy. The life of the Church is not confined to clerical contributions, but all members of the Church are involved in this. Pastoral theology, therefore, can no longer be limited to the pastoral functions of the clergy. It must become "practical theology" in the true sense of the word.

This implies two conditions. On the one hand, it must take account of all members and all functions which, in one way or another, contribute to the self-realization of the Church. On the other hand, it must subject the constantly changing contemporary situation to an equally constant theological and sociological analysis. This is vital because the contemporary situation is precisely that moment of salvation history in which God makes *us* here and now responsible for the realization of the Church. Only when this contemporary situation is analyzed and interpreted as exactly as possible can pastoral theology develop the principles and imperative decisions required by the Church for its action now and in the future. Only then, too, can the Church begin to plan its attitude toward the contemporary world and will it be able to guide, organize and coordinate its activities, and all that is implied, on every level, from top to bottom.

The basis of all the problems put forth and all the results of research to be published in the pastoral section of CONCILIUM is that pastoral theology is here understood as "practical theology" in the sense outlined above. The intention is therefore not, even in this pastoral domain, to provide a textbook of pastoral theology in installments, but rather to deal with such decisive issues as are beyond the capacity of the individual pastoral theologian. For example, how often has pastoral activity in the Church always the character of service? Or, how far can the Church plan its activities? What is the state of the Church's contribution to developing countries? What kind of situations has the Church to deal with in various continents, countries or racial groups? This section should deal, above all, with conclusions reached by practical-theological research; with the analysis of the contemporary situation; with the relationship between kerygma and dogma, etc.

In this way CONCILIUM will serve a twofold purpose: to provide worldwide information and to achieve cooperation and coordination. Both are indispensable. Planning the self-realization of the Church involves not only individual parishes, but also dioceses, groups of dioceses and the Church as a whole.

PART I

ARTICLES

Heinz Schuster/ *Saarbrücken, W. Germany*

The Nature and Function
of Pastoral Theology

The problem of the nature and function of pastoral theology as a theological science has become the more pressing as today the Church's pastoral activity finds itself in a state of perplexity in various ways. There is, of course, no necessary connection between pastoral activity and pastoral theology in the sense that the efficacy of pastoral activity is by no means guaranteed by the exact, scientific systematization of pastoral theology. On the other hand, theory and practice are interdependent in principle, and the growing perplexity that reigns in pastoral theology as a theological science is without doubt a feature of the perplexity that reigns in the Church's pastoral care itself.

It is beyond the scope of this brief article to treat, even in part, of the historical reasons—whether we take the history of ideas or of theology—that led to the problem of the place of pastoral theology in the scientific theory of theology as a whole and to the problem of its specific theological function. Questions concerning these problems have been brought up again and again but for a long time remained without a coherent and fully satis-

* HEINZ SCHUSTER: Born May 12, 1930 in Rübenbach/Kreis, Coblenz, Germany. He was ordained in 1955 for the Diocese of Trier, W. Germany, and earned his doctorate in theology at the University of Innsbruck under Karl Rahner.

fying answer.[1] In any case, it is true that the relatively young discipline of pastoral theology only[2] meant to fill a gap in clerical training and not in theological thought as a whole. Therefore, it already had a place in the syllabus of Catholic theology before theology itself had made proper room for it. Basically, pastoral theology meant a course in which the individual "pastor" was given directives for his pastoral practice.[3] As its name indicates, this course addressed itself to the individual priest, and its theme was his practical activity. This narrow and even clerical concept of pastoral theology was strongly criticized by Catholic theologians of Tübingen as early as the middle of the 19th century.[4] An effort was made to expand pastoral theology into a "practical theology" that would have as its object the communal self-formation of the Church in the present and the future.[5] Yet, pastoral theology clung to its own unecclesiological outlook until well into the 20th century. To this we must add that the one pastoral theology that originally contained all the questions about the pastoral function of the individual priest, and all the forms and norms of actual pastoral care, was split up into various separate

[1] A full treatment of these questions of history and scientific theory may be found in F. X. Arnold, K. Rahner, V. Schurr and L. M. Weber, *Handbuch der Pastoraltheologie. Praktische Theologie der Kirche in ihrer Gegenwart*, Vol. I (Freiburg, 1964), pp. 40-111. This manual represents the first attempt to work out a strict theologico-ecclesiological concept of pastoral theology as a practical theology of the Church's contemporary self-fulfillment with the assistance of well-known collaborators in the most varied fields of professional practical theology. It is based on K. Rahner's *Plan und Aufrisz eines Handbuches der Pastoraltheologie* (printed as a ms. Freiburg, 1960).

[2] It became an independent subject in theological colleges in the German-speaking field when Maria Theresa reorganized theological studies in 1777, and so it became recognized as an autonomous discipline in the universities.

[3] This was the case in all textbooks of pastoral theology until the middle of the 19th century, and then again until well into the 20th century. Cf. for example, F. C. Pittroff, *Anleitung zur praktischen Gottes Gelehrtheit*, 4 Vols. (Prague, 1779-84); A. Reichenberger, *Pastoralanweisung nach den Bedürfnissen unseres Zeitalters* (Vienna, 1805-8); but see also C. Krieg, *Die Wissenschaft der speziellen Seelenführung* (Freiburg, 1904).

[4] Cf. A. Graf, *Kritische Darstellung des gegenwärtigen Zustandes der praktischen Theologie* (Tübingen, 1841).

[5] A. Graf, *op. cit.*, p. 5 and p. 125.

disciplines such as pastoral liturgy, catechetics, homiletics, and later, pastoral medicine, pastoral sociology, etc. These disciplines, indeed, pursue the same pragmatic purpose, the training of the priest, but their basic cohesion becomes more and more blurred because they all have their own research work, method and presentation.

In today's search for the nature and specific function of pastoral theology there appear several demands and assumptions that are already treated in systematic theology or in ecclesiology and cannot be overlooked in a new approach to pastoral theology. We can only roughly and briefly summarize the more important ones:

1. Christ's redemption is not only carried on by the pastoral activity of the individual priest, but by all members of the Church.

2. The active life of the Church cannot, therefore, be split up into the pastoral activity of the clerical functions in the Church on the one hand, and on the other, the passive function of the led, guided and cared-for flock. Pastoral theology should not simply give the impression that the life of the Church wholly depends on the regulations, norms and rubrics that govern the activity of the individual priest. Historical and systematic theology has taught us that the nature and function of the Church is to continue the redemption of man through the grace of God. There is, therefore, apart from dogmatic theology, exegesis, an ecclesiology dealing with the Church as such and also necessarily a "practical theology". It follows, then, that if we wish to deal with the practical, "pastoral" problem of how to work out all this in the concrete, we must accept the fact that the whole Church with all those that represent it and all its functions is the object of this pastoral theology.[6]

3. This Church has no God-given infallible knowledge about

---

[6] For this, see particularly the studies by F. X. Arnold, *Grundsäzliches und Geschichtliches zur Theologie der Seelsorge* (Freiburg, 1949), and *Seelsorge aus der Mitte der Heilsgeschichte* (Freiburg, 1956).

the structure of the contemporary society where she has to proclaim her message, fulfill her task and so reach her own fulfillment. This contemporary society, with all that it implies, is not a mere passing moment in this self-fulfillment of the Church, but is willed and ordered as such by God himself. The Church, therefore, cannot behave as if she is not, or is hardly, touched by these ever new contemporary tendencies; as if the constant cultural, sociological and aesthetic changes brought about in the course of human history were but a change of decor in front of which she plays her invariable act, untouched by it all, according to eternal rules and always with the same texts. Since the actual life of the Church is conditioned by the contemporary situation and the Church has no infallible insight into the features of this situation, she will have to analyze and interpret this situation theologically before she can proceed with that self-fulfillment as presented here and now. But what branch of theology can deal with this task, basic to the effectiveness of the Church's life, except pastoral theology? [7]

These three points seem to us mainly to dominate the principal demands made for some time by theologians belonging to the most varied schools and to very different regions. Hence, it is possible to define pastoral theology as *that branch of theology which deals with the Church's self-fulfillment in the ever new contemporary situation*. This definition is still general. To clarify it the following points must be much more closely investigated: (1) the scope of what it covers, or the subject matter of pastoral

[7] It is evident, in contrast with other branches of theology, that pastoral theology has always had a certain flair for contemporary needs and for the applicability of norms laid down by canon law, the rubrics, the liturgy, etc. But here we rather mean, as will be explained further on, that the contemporary situation is seen in principle and positively as the situation in which the Church's activity takes place, and, therefore, as an aspect of her self-fulfillment in the present. As such, it becomes the specific, formal viewpoint in the light of which pastoral theology considers its subject matter, the Church's fulfillment, methodically and systematically; this provides pastoral theology with a function that demands its own scientific theory, which springs from the very nature of the Church, and which no other branch of theology treats.

theology; (2) the specific angle from which this subject matter is viewed, worked out and presented; (3) its specific method and (4) the aim of a pastoral theology understood in this sense.[8]

The subject matter of pastoral theology is not, as its name might seem to imply, the "pastor" or the pastoral function of the clergy, but the Church itself, and as a whole. In contrast with basic ecclesiology, which deals principally with the enduring transcendental and sacramental nature of the Church, pastoral theology deals with the Church as a dynamic entity, with a communal structure and subject to the vicissitudes of history; an entity that must express itself here and now in present actuality in order to be concretely what it ought to be, and to do concretely what it ought to do. Pastoral theology can, therefore, rightly be called "existential ecclesiology", especially when one considers that its special task is to work out and to formulate the principles and urgent duties that the Church needs for her contemporary fulfillment—a point that will be developed further on.

If, however, the Church as a whole is the subject matter of pastoral theology, then it must treat of each of the following points:

(a) All those who cooperate in the Church's fulfillment; the various functions and positions of all the members who share in the Church's self-development and in her work of transmitting salvation. These members include the individual Christian, the individual Church community, the various functionaries of the Church, the bishops and their dioceses, and even the pope and the Roman Curia.

(b) All basic activities through which the Church fulfills her task, including the preaching of the Word, the liturgy and worship of the Church, the way she lives in each of the sacraments,

[8] I point out once more that the term "pastoral theology" taken literally only refers to the pastoral activity of the individual "pastor". But this meaning is today no longer tenable as has been shown here briefly, and, I hope, clearly. In German the term "practical theology" suggested itself as it has long been current here; it is pertinent, and does not so easily lead to an unecclesiological misunderstanding of our subject. Cf. my article "Praktische Theologie," in *Lexikon für Theologie und Kirche*, VIII, 2nd ed. (Freiburg, 1963), cc. 682-5.

the practice of Christian love, the Christian life of the individual faithful, insofar as all these factors contain definite expressions of the Church's life.

(c) All the communal and sociological aspects of the Church's nature and activity, since these are most liable to structural changes.

(d) And last but not least, the formal basic lines along which this fulfillment takes place in the Church: the various kinds of piety; the difference of the sexes and its significance for the actual life of the Church; the various tensions between theory and practice in the moral life of the individual Christian, as well as between the provision, administration, assimilation and personal fulfillment of that salvation that is present in the Church and must be constantly operative in adaptation to variety in fulfillment.

If we understand the subject matter of pastoral theology in this comprehensive way, then the various branches of practical theology, such as liturgy, catechetics, homiletics, missiology, the study of practical charity, etc., become in the end, parts of the one pastoral theology. This does not, however, decide the question how far these subdivisions need their own research and their own presentation by specialists.

The formal aspect from which the subject matter of pastoral theology as outlined above must be seen and dealt with is the way in which the contemporary situation constantly conditions this fulfillment of the Church. There is no doubt that pastoral theology has always shown interest in the needs of the time and the changes in certain pastoral assumptions, etc. But its clerical origin restricted this interest to the situation of the individual "pastor" and his pastoral activity. The contemporary reality and its concomitant social and cultural changes were mainly considered as superficial, refractory matter that free pastoral care must oppose and must change, and if necessary, against its will, with the help of traditional forms and tactics, in such a way that it fits in with the accustomed, "unchanging" image of the Church.

Pastoral theology, however, as meant here, can only see every contemporary situation as God's ineluctable call to the Church, wherein he reminds her of her ever new and ever actual tasks, and addresses himself to her ever again as his free partner, as the ever historical and changing situation in which alone God's free self-communication to man can take place. Insofar as the Church is concerned with herself and her permanent mission, and insofar as she must accept the God-given conditions of salvation as it penetrates history, and through history approaches the individual human person, she is bound to concern herself with the concrete historical situation as implied in her mission and her actual fulfillment. How this concern must be treated by and in pastoral theology is, finally, a matter of theological method.

First of all, there can be no doubt that the above-mentioned definition of the formal object of pastoral theology has already largely indicated the place of this study in theology as a whole. This becomes still clearer when we briefly consider the question in the light of scientific theory. It is obvious that the historical sciences treat of the Church's past as a theological subject; it is equally obvious that the permanent nature of the Church and of God's salvation, present and operative in her, constitutes a theological subject, namely, in dogmatic theology and biblical science. A genuinely theological, methodical and scientific treatment of the Church as a contemporary phenomenon has so far remained mainly an unfulfilled wish. This problem is not solved by the mere fact that considerations of pastoral activity have shown increasing interest in sociological questions or in the structural changes of contemporary society. For understandable psychological reasons that have been indicated above, this interest arose mainly when it became apparent that one could hardly approach this new world with the traditional forms and norms of pastoral activity. This interest showed, therefore, an outlook that was basically defensive rather than constructive; it was not really concerned with the Church as such or with a decisive moment in her self-fulfillment, but was rather the fortuitous and private concern of some of her functionaries, and this concern could hardly be considered binding for the Church or for some vital sector of her life.

What is decisive for the proposed formal object of pastoral theology is that it is based on the nature of the Church and is, therefore, indispensable. This means that it is also indispensable for her theology. And this, in turn, already implies a decisive point concerning method in pastoral theology: the foregoing thoughts about the contemporary situation cannot be limited to a secular sociological analysis. This situation can only be rightly understood against the background of the will of God, already embodied, permanently and historically, in the Church and, therefore, alive in the Church's self-knowledge, at least in its main features. Particular sociological problems are, therefore, determined and formulated by the Church and her theological self-awareness. Contemporary history, indeed, is a necessary aspect of the enduring and transcendental Church in the concrete and as such is significant for the actual self-fulfillment of the Church.

A merely secular sociography and sociology could never provide the Church with a decisive and binding answer to such crucial questions of pastoral theology as those concerning the actual structure of the Church (its government, its regional divisions, the kind and manner in which it fashions the community, its relation to the secular societies and cultural institutions of a modern State, the concrete forms, words and signs used in its self-fulfillment, its preaching, its religious instruction, the administration of its sacraments, etc.), and how far all this is a necessary consequence of its permanent nature, or rather, of its experimental situation or of its pilgrim condition, which is beyond control as well as beyond an ultimately satisfactory explanation and can only be accepted with patience, or perhaps with a blind and guilty hardening of the manifestations and features of its life. And it is precisely these questions that must be answered before the Church can proceed, with the help of pastoral theology, to lay down principles and decisions for her work in the contemporary situation.

In particular, we may perhaps distinguish three groups of questions that must belong to the theological and sociological analysis of pastoral theology as here understood:

(a) Those questions that concern the situation and structure of the present world as a whole, because the Church has become a world-Church as never before. She can only understand her specific mission in the light of this total world. Only when she recognizes the tendencies and basic structures of the contemporary world, can she plan her mission to the world on a truly strategic basis, and that she can and must do to a large degree in a methodical and scientific fashion, without rejecting the charismatic initiative of individual persons or particular missionary societies and orders.

(b) Those questions that concern the situation and structure of societies within the world; for the Church, whether she likes it or not, is in the eyes of the world one religious society and one religious institution among many others. Among these, however, she has an undoubted, privileged place of which she must be fully conscious before she can truly occupy it. With these other religious societies the Church shares, *e.g.*, the problem of religious liberty, of tolerance, of world peace, of the universal human ethos, etc.

(c) Those questions that concern the situation of the individual person in the present world, insofar as the individual is always already integrated in the secular society and is always first to undergo any change in the social structure. This group of questions might seem the most urgent in ordinary pastoral activity. But, as has already been said, it would be fundamentally wrong to prize the individual situation out of the total situation of the Church. The result would in any case be merely a matter of pastoral tactics, but not part of the strategy of the overall self-fulfillment of the Church in the present situation, which ought to be the proper purpose of pastoral theology.

In conclusion, we must briefly examine the aim of pastoral theology as here understood. The primary aim of this branch of theology is, as should be sufficiently clear by now, to plan the fulfillment of the Church for the present and the future. In this, it differs sharply from that kind of pastoral theology whose main concern is the training and practical preparation of the individual "pastor". This practical and pragmatic preparation for the ministry will, of course, always keep its place in the training of the future clergy, but as such it is not quite what is meant here by pastoral theology.

We might possibly admit that the theological branch that deals with the fulfillment of the Church as contemporary could perhaps better be called "practical theology".[9] Yet both are closely connected as seems obvious: practical theology as such can but provide a basis for a scientifically responsible self-awareness of the Church as she has to act here and now; it can also work out principles and decisions for the contemporary fulfillment of the Church; however, in itself, it is not yet the pastoral concern and activity of the Church proper. It cannot take the place of a pastoral conference at which the clergy, for instance, give counsel on the needs of a specific area of the Church; what must be done here and now, or how far certain practical theological principles can bind, or be applied to, this area; nor can it ignore a concrete application of its general knowledge by an individual Church member who must here and now represent or "realize" the Church, in the way dogmatic theology can ignore the fact that an individual preacher uses a specific theological theory about satisfaction for an acceptable, credible sermon. Pastoral theology in the proposed sense is, therefore, strictly a theological and, moreover, a somewhat theoretical study. But without solid theory, solid practice is impossible.

It is obvious that what has been said so far is only a rough and ready outline of what could and should be said about the nature and function of pastoral theology. Particularly, nothing has been said yet about the fact that this concept of pastoral theology does away with the relative exclusiveness and the tendency to generalize that beset so many questions dealt with by theology at large. One has to take into account that what may

[9] See previous footnote, p. 8.

be important and deserving of careful investigation from the point of view of pastoral theology in one particular area of the Church, may be unimportant and hardly theologically significant in another. The pluralistic structures and tendencies of contemporary society do not allow either the Church as a whole or the individual active member to expect that the laws governing Christian practice are always already understood by the hierarchy or that they can be decided by a simple act of authority, or that, when such laws have at last been discovered, they are generally valid for every other area of the Church or for every other phase of its history.

This does not mean, however, that in the future we have to deal with a whole variety of pastoral theologies, each one of which is authoritative for its own area and, because of that, would prevent any overall planning of the Church's fulfillment. Differences and particular measures can be significant and necessary without having to lead to a confused, uncoordinated multiplicity of theological endeavor. Our kind of pastoral theology rather provides a scientific and theological meeting-ground. Here the manifold considerations, analyses, experiments and theories of the highest authorities in the Church as well as of the various theological research establishments, the various pastoral organizations, and, not least, the many individual pastoral theologians can be brought together. Here all can be sorted out, coordinated and carefully considered in the light of one common purpose, namely, the self-fulfillment of the Church as it is necessary here and now.

In spite of all this, we cannot overlook the essentially contingent nature of such planning of this overall fulfillment by pastoral theology. One should rather accept this fact in a positive manner. The Church reflecting upon her own contemporary presence and future, must submit this planning to the essentially hidden providence of God, steer clear of every kind of this-worldly utopia and of every kind of ecclesiastical planning commission that might attempt to foresee and prearrange everything in an *a priori* misrepresentation of true pastoral care.

Karl Rahner, S.J./ *Munich, W. Germany*

Observations on Episcopacy in the Light of Vatican II

There can be no doubt that the dogmatic Constitution on the Church is the most significant achievement of Vatican Council II insofar as the immediately practical results of the Council are concerned. Within this Constitution, the teaching on episcopacy in chapter III is the most important. This does not mean that the rest of the Constitution is but framework and decoration. It is, indeed, possible that at some later time other things will derive their full meaning for the Church and the world from this Constitution, *e.g.*, with regard to the salvation of all men, including those outside the Church. But the very length and relevance of the conciliar debates on this chapter already show that the Council itself considered this its most important contribution.

* KARL RAHNER, S.J.: Born March 5, 1904 in Freiburg-im-Breisgau, Germany, he became a Jesuit in 1922. He studied philosophy at Pullach, Germany, taught at Feldkirch, Austria, studied theology at Valenburg, Netherlands and was ordained in 1932. In 1937 he became a lecturer in Innsbruck, Vienna and Pullach, and in 1948 professor of dogma at the Leopold-Franzens University in Innsbruck. After numerous theological writings (in which is expressed his central idea: an anthropocentric conception of the whole of theology), Rahner has come to be recognized more and more as one of the most important theological thinkers of the German-speaking world. At present he is professor of Christian thought at the University of Munich. His students have compiled a bibliography of his various writings which number nearly 300 essays.

This conciliar teaching has important theologico-pastoral consequences both in itself and in the conclusions indicated in the Constitution. The following observations bear on this point. As this is only a brief article, we may disregard those parts of chapter III on the hierarchy dealing with either the pope or the already known specific functions of the individual bishop as priest, teacher and shepherd of his diocese, or those parts dealing directly with the individual priest or deacon.

The teaching on episcopacy in the Constitution may be very briefly summarized. Jesus Christ left to his Church a hierarchical structure, *i.e.*, he gave it functions of sacred power (understood as service) that belong in the first instance to the bishops, as successors of the apostles under the pope, who is the visible principle and foundation of episcopal unity (n. 18). The apostles, selected as Church leaders, already form a "collegium" according to the will of Christ (n. 19). Their successors are *ex divina institutione* the bishops with and under the pope (n. 20). Episcopal ordination by imposition of hands is a true sacrament in which the bishops receive the plenitude of their functions, although they can discharge these in view of their teaching and pastoral functions only in the unity of the whole Church (n. 21). Just as the apostles formed a "college" as ordained by Christ, so the bishops form a true "college". This college exists in the possession of its authority only insofar as it is united with, and led by, the bishop of Rome by reason of his supreme authority as defined by Vatican Council I.

Forming such a college, however, the bishops share collectively in the plenitude of power in the Church. Granted that a collegial action takes place in cooperation with the pope, this authority can be exercised by the college of bishops either within or outside the context of an ecumenical council. Membership in this college depends on episcopal ordination and union with the head and members of this college (n. 22). The individual bishop as such is, therefore, not only the authoritative leader of his own diocese, but has, as a member of the college and according to Christ's institution and command, also a responsibility (not jurisdiction) and function for the whole Church where the unity of the Church's faith and life, as well as her missionary activity, are concerned. This unity of the college and its function is manifested in practice (although subject to historical circumstances) in the larger units of the Church, such as patriarchates, and today also in episcopal conferences (n. 23).

What is the significance of this conciliar teaching on episcopacy in terms of pastoral theology? First of all, insofar as the practical and more difficult application of this teaching is concerned, the Constitution clearly rejects the idea so prevalent among laity and clergy alike, though not often brought to the surface, that the bishop is but a kind of subordinate officer of the pope. The bishop rules his flock by his own (not delegated) ordinary authority in the name of Christ and not in that of the pope (n. 27). This does not conflict with the fact that he must guide his flock in unity with, and under, the authority of the supreme power in the Church. The bishop has received his pastoral function in its *fullness* and in its normal form (*habitualis et cotidiana cura*) (n. 27). He cannot consider himself as the mere transmitter and executor of commands from higher quarters. He cannot shirk his own function and responsibility. He would, therefore, not fulfill his duty completely if he looked on his function merely as the application of general laws of the Church or of initiatives sent from Rome. Whether as an individual bishop or in a regional episcopal conference he must try to find out for himself the scope of his task and the hour of his action; he himself must decide, show initiative and discover imperative solutions that are not the mere application of general norms provided by canon law and pastoral theology. Only in this way can his diocese and the fulfillment of his task lead to the good of "the whole body" of the Church (n. 23); for the Church is not a homogeneous mass, but an organic structure that can only claim *universalitas* through the real differences (*varietas*) of its members (nn. 13, 22, 23).

The conciliar declaration that the sacramental ordination of the bishop confers all three offices of teacher, priest and shepherd, will cause the canonists many headaches. For it is not easily reconcilable with the already old traditional teaching that there are two basic powers (that of order and pastoral power: *potestas ordinis* and *potestas iurisdictionis*), of which the power of jurisdiction is not transmitted through (under the circumstances, absolute) ordination but through canonical mission.

This is not the place to deal fully with this point, but the fact that the Council puts the foundation of the whole office in the sacrament, and, therefore, in the *pneuma*, has an incalculable significance for canonical practice in the Church. Justice and love, law and brotherliness, charisma and institution, can in the future no longer be treated simply as identical, because in spite of man's pneumatic oneness they are not the same in his pluralistic condition, and the distinction serves this unity. But the very fact that the law is rooted in the *pneuma* makes it clear that law in the Church is no worldly law but a law that is sacred and inspired by the Spirit, an embodiment of grace, and that its exercise is only conformed to the will of Christ when its application is inspired by this spirit, the spirit of humility, of the will to serve, of brotherliness, of respect for every single person and his conscience, of self-criticism and of the authority's will to accept advice and new experience, of the *affectus collegialis* that the bishop must show toward his priests, of the will to work together with his priests whom he should consider as his friends (cf. nn. 27, 28). Canon law must be inspired by the Spirit of Christ, for only then can it be called the law of the Church of Christ.

The Council maintains that the one, whole office, sacramentally conferred on the bishop in its triple unfolding, is lawfully divided in the Church *vario gradu, variis subiectis* (priests, deacons) (n. 28). Even if this does not decide the question in the history of dogma, whether Christ himself willed the three levels of the one *ordo* or whether they result from a lawful decision made by the apostolic Church, it nevertheless points to the dogmatic basis of a way of thinking and an attitude that are important from the pastoral point of view. The almost incredible multiplicity of offices, functions, authoritative bodies and institutions of the hierarchical Church—which often look almost secular and as if shaped through outward circumstances—must all be seen as rooted in the pneumatic oneness of the sacrament of the episcopal and priestly office. Every office in the Church must be understood in the Spirit as the concrete expression of the sacramental mystery of the *ordo,* or, where this is no longer seriously possible, should be handed over to lay people who can perform the function just as well or better.

The conciliar teaching on episcopacy clearly indicates (n. 23) that the institution of patriarchates, Church provinces and episcopal conferences is the application of the collegial structure of the Church, though subject to historical circumstance and, formally, a human institution. The subject of episcopal conferences is far too important to give here the treatment it deserves. Moreover, it must also first become clearer how this institution will develop canonically after the Council. One can only hope that the *collegialis affectus* will find here a genuine *concreta applicatio* (n. 23), *i.e.,* that these conferences will acquire the canonical shape and spirit demanded by the pastoral situation of the individual countries and continents, so that throughout the world there really will be Churches that can act on their own responsibility and are not exclusively dependent on Rome and its nuncios for representation, leadership and full responsibility as units of the Church.

In the long run, there will inevitably be certain cases where the individual bishop will be legally bound by the decision of an episcopal conference. Such conferences will also have to guide interdiocesan organizations and institutions such as charitable organizations, film institutes, etc., which present-day pastoral care needs without question. The same holds for new divisions of dioceses and Church provinces: it is essential that the episcopal conferences do their work.

A further conclusion (by human right in the present situation of the Church) follows from the collegiality of the bishops among themselves and with the pope as head of the college: the pope must be supported in the guidance of the universal Church by representatives of the bishops from the whole Church. This, of course, should not lead to a permanent Council, since such co-operation would not mean a collegial act of all the bishops together. Nor is this demand satisfied by the episcopal character of many officials of the Curia. It is rather a matter of representatives of the bishops throughout the *world*. Nor should such bishops reside permanently in Rome. They would only become themselves officials of the Roman Curia or *chargés d'affaires* for bishops or episcopal conferences without their own initiative and responsibility. (This does not prevent bishops from being in addition also members of some Roman body, although they would not, presumably, be permanently residing in Rome.) From the nature of the case, they should be episcopal representatives of the bishops' conferences, chosen by these conferences, in order to meet in Rome at regular intervals and to constitute there an advisory body to the pope. This advisory board would thus have priority over the curial executive since it would be immediately attached to the pope as the one who is responsible for legislation in the Church. If this episcopal advisory board, desired by the Council, were set up in this way, it would already have taken care of a major part of the curial reform, which Pope Paul VI has already declared himself in favor of at the beginning of his pontificate, and which is also the wish of the Council.

Although the Constitution on the Church does not explicitly deal with the actual size of a diocese, it implicitly provides the basis on which to decide this thorny question. A diocese is governed directly by a member of the highest governing body of the Church, and not by some subordinate official of this body. Insofar as the size of a diocese is concerned, this implies an upper limit in that the essence of the Church must be able to stand out clearly, and a lower limit in that it must be large enough for the bishop to be able to exercise his function in a genuine way. If, now and in the future, a diocese presents a situation where it cannot somehow represent the life and fulfillment of the whole Church in its various dimensions and make it truly actual, it is not a "Church" in the full sense of the word and does not qualify for direct government by a member of the highest governing body of the Church. The practical application of this principle will of course be influenced by demographic, social, psychological, economic, geographical and historical circumstances. But all this does not take away from its theologico-pastoral significance. It can hardly be doubted that the resolute application of this principle must lead to the merging of many very small dioceses. But it is also clear that the lower limit, which is based on the nature of episcopacy, also demands the division of dioceses that are too large.

When one reflects upon the Council's teaching on episcopacy, a problem arises that is partly dogmatic, partly theologico-pastoral, and not easy to formulate. Perhaps it could be called the problem of the relationship and the tension between the legal and the real structures of the Church. This needs explaining. In the Constitution on the Church the bishop (the pope not included here) appears as *the* shepherd of a Church, without qualification: in *him* lies the fullness of all sacred power, *he* preaches, *he* teaches, *he* consecrates and *he* guides the Church's people entrusted to him. All functional activity of the Church in the transmission of truth and grace is concentrated in him.

One might object that such a description is highly unrealistic. In reality, the bishop is a kind of superior official who can only supervise and coordinate the real activity of the Church; and the proper and essential activity of the Church—her true pastoral care, her preaching (kerygma), her word of grace in the sacraments, her witness to Christ in the face of the world—(insofar as it is a matter of office) is in reality borne by the priests of the parish. One might object that the Council's version of the bishop's office looks like an *a priori* notion, unreal, and does not reflect the original and real view of the Church's reality. (One might add that this problem is also an ecumenical and theologically controversial one: the theology of the evangelical Churches views the offices of the Church as based primarily on the actual preaching of the Gospel in the concrete community by the pastor, and so can only see the "bishop" as a necessary "superintendent" of this life in the concrete community.)

One might, of course, answer that the Council deals clearly and extensively with the importance of the individual parochial clergy as the bishop's assistants, as real priests and as leaders of the concrete community (particularly as gathered around the altar). One might even add that the Council has brought out the essence of the concrete community (around the altar, local Church, parish) as a true "Church", in which *the* Church becomes real and present in the world, in a way in which it has never appeared before in doctrinal documents; a teaching of which the theologico-pastoral consequences can hardly be foreseen as yet, as it really provides a basis for a *theology* of the parish, and not merely for its place in canon law. Yet, in our opinion, this does not quite solve the theological and pastoral problem. This requires a further and closer development of the theology of the local and eucharistic community as manifestation and actual realization of the Church as such in concrete space and time, and this theology must be made vital and fruitful in the life of the individual community.

One might say that, as long as the local community is not yet existentially, in thought, in deed and in faith, conscious of being a Church, to which all that the Council said about the glory and mystery of *the* Church applies; as long as the individual community still sees itself as the smallest administrative unit through which the whole Church looks only after the salvation of the individual, it does not truly understand itself. There are things to be done here that are pastorally most important for the life of the individual communities and for the full and true organization of this life, without which the episcopal Church, too, is not what it ought to be.

In order to understand in the full theological sense the tension between the episcopal Church and the local Church, the relationship has to be further investigated. It was no problem in the early Church since every true local Church was a bishop's Church. Likewise, during the Middle Ages and thereafter the problem in the West could not be properly resolved: the local Church did not experience its existence as "Church" so that its institutions were felt in the Church as presenting no difficulties and based on simply human right that can be arranged freely according to sound judgment. If, however, the local Church is truly recognized as Church, then its concrete shape may be subject to change and historical circumstances; but insofar as this concrete shape expresses the *essence* of the Church it must show *iure divino* what *the* Church is, so that a Christian can truly experience *here* what is meant by "Church": the sacramental presence of God's deifying and forgiving grace and the unity of mankind in love.

When this empirical reality of the Church is truly present and experienced in the local community, then the Christian can also experience in his religious life the episcopal nature of the Church, which lies, as it were, on a deeper level in the organism of the Church, and which no longer gives the impression of being a mere abstract theory that has nothing to do with the concrete life of the Church.

* NOTE: For a more penetrating theological study of this problem, see K. Rahner/J. Ratzinger, *The Episcopate and the Primacy* (New York: Herder and Herder, 1964); K. Rahner, "Zur Theologie der Pfarrei," in H. Rahner, *Die Pfarre* (Freiburg im Breisgau, 1956), pp. 27-36; *idem,* "Uber den Begriff des 'ius divinum' im katholischen Verständniss," in *Schriften zur Theologie* V (Einsiedlen, 1962), pp. 249-77; *idem,* "Uber den Episkopat," in *Stimmen der Zeit* 173 (1963), pp. 161-95; *idem,* "Dogmatische Fragen des Konzils," in *Oberrheinisches Pastoralblatt* 64 (1963), pp. 234-50.

François Houtart / *Brussels, Belgium*

Walter Goddijn, O.F.M. / *Rotterdam, Netherlands*

Problems of Pastoral Organization

I t is still too early to attempt a synthesis of the new thinking that has been done in the field of comprehensive pastoral care and pastoral projects. We can, however, look at the reasons that led to this new thinking and at the aims it pursues.

THE ORIGIN OF THIS NEW THINKING

For the first part of this study I shall not distinguish between comprehensive pastoral care and pastoral projects, since the basic ideas are more or less the same for both. The distinction will be taken up later on.

Two main points seem to have prompted this development. The first was the realization that in spite of the heroic efforts made by priests, religious and lay people, the results have been

* FRANÇOIS HOUTART: Born March 7, 1925 in Brussels, Belgium, he was ordained in 1949 for the Diocese of Malines-Brussels. Studied political and social sciences at the University of Louvain, urbanology at the Institut Supérieur d'Urbanisme Appliqué in Brussels, and pursued further studies at the University of Chicago. At present he is working toward his doctorate at the University of Louvain. He has been director of the Centre de Recherches Socio-religieuses, and secretary of the Conférence Internationale de Sociologie Religieuse since 1956. His many articles on religious sociology, urban sociology and pastoral subjects have appeared in periodicals around the world.

very meager, whether in the evangelization of the developing countries or in the more thorough christianization of those that were evangelized long ago.

Pope Pius drew attention to this in 1955 when, speaking to Lenten preachers in Rome, he said: "When one sees, on the one hand, the enthusiasm of so many undertakings in which no one halts or slackens his pace or spares himself, and, on the other, is forced to recognize that the results obtained are at the expense of so much energy and so much self-denial, one wonders whether some perhaps struggle too much alone, too individualistically and disunited. Would it not be better, dear sons, if apostolic activity . . . were reexamined in the light of the principles that govern all orderly collaboration? In my opinion, this is today one of the most urgent needs of the apostolic action of clergy and laity in our day."

The second point is the discovery of new fields of pastoral care and of new dimensions in the old ones. The problems thrown up by the changing society in which we live have become too complex. The areas of specialization in our collective society, the mobility of the population, the disintegration of the basic communities of village or small neighborhood, all require new knowledge, new apostolic organization, new forms of activity. Yet, almost everywhere in the Church we still live with a pastoral individualism, inherited from the era of liberalism and affecting both parishes and dioceses. On the other hand, new areas of similar pastoral activity have sprung up gradually where education, labor or the family are concerned, but there is lack of integration.

These two points, therefore, show the need for a pastoral activity that is better coordinated and incorporates the new fields of action and the new dimensions.

COMPREHENSIVE PASTORAL CARE AND PASTORAL PROJECTS

It might be of interest to examine these two concepts in their historical context. The first arose in France and its principal protagonists were Canon Boulard and Father Motte, O.F.M.

There was a dynamism in pastoral activity that led to various new approaches. There was also a certain inadequacy in the renewal of individual parishes, and there was a lack of integration of wider missionary activity with the pastoral work of the parish. Thus, the idea of comprehensive pastoral care grew, little by little. Regional "missions", *i.e.*, missions covering a geographical unit like a town or a rural district, helped considerably to bring greater precision to the idea and to the methods of applying it.

A certain number of dioceses took this as a starting-point and organized themselves accordingly, particularly by dividing their territory into zones based on typical common features. The idea spread and was adopted outside France in Belgium, Italy, Spain and Canada, while in Germany and the Netherlands independent but similar efforts took shape.

In contrast to comprehensive pastoral care, the idea of pastoral projects started in developing countries, particularly in Latin America and Africa. Examples will be given later on. It no doubt owes its origin to the parallel movement of development projects. As we know, such a project consists in examining all the elements required for economic and social development, and then in co-ordinating the various elements available in the present situation in order to get the most out of them for this purpose. They have realized, above all, how few means they have at their disposal to attain this end.

In the same way, a pastoral project consists in assessing the factors of a region, diocese or country that can be used to cope with evangelization, and then to see how to direct them so that they fully answer the various needs of time and place.

It should be clear now that comprehensive pastoral care and pastoral projects have much in common. No serious attempt has been made yet to define the differences. Insofar as the facts are concerned one could compare the pastoral projects of the developing countries with the methods of the "community *development*", and comprehensive pastoral care with "community *organization*". This is why pastoral projects were first mentioned in countries where apostolic activity has to take place in a situation of rapid social change. This demands original solutions and often requires a complete recasting of the Church's organization and activity. In contrast, in countries where ecclesial organization and activity are more dense and where social changes are less radical, it will be mainly a matter of coordination in order to harness a truly communal effort.

Yet, more precision is necessary. A first distinction was provided by Canon Boulard in a note to CELAM.* On the one hand, the Church must plan with the methods that are customary in these matters: pastoral organizations, commissions and advisors, programs for study and action. She must use these as effectively as possible with due regard to the cultural needs of time and place. On the other hand, the Church must actively remain the "light of Christ" in the world. She must, therefore, always remain at the service of the Gospel and the world, while remaining one in herself. Therefore, Canon Boulard suggests that the first type of action should be called a "plan for pastoral organization" or "plan for ecclesial development", and the second type should be called "principles of pastoral advancement" or "principles of pastoral direction". These two types each call for a different systematic approach to pastoral care. Moreover, in one form or other this distinction occurs in all the official documents that national hierarchies have devoted to comprehensive pastoral care.

Lastly, a distinction has been made between "program" and "plan", insofar as pastoral work is concerned. In some Western countries, particularly in Italy and Belgium, politicians are frightened by the word "planning" because to them it is too closely connected with Communist systems of government. Yet, the ideas must keep their objective meaning. For pastoral organization, then, the word "program" has been used to define the objectives in view, and the word "plan" for the ways and means of reaching them.[1]

* Latin American Episcopal Conference.
[1] L. Dingemans and F. Houtart, *Pastorale d'une région industrielle* (Brussels: CEP, 1964), pp. 113-4.

As can be seen, the vocabulary is far from being fixed. Its very diversity shows how new the problem is. It is, therefore, interesting to note that Pope Pius XII laid down the conditions of comprehensive pastoral work when he addressed the Lenten preachers in Rome, and that Pope John XXIII used the idea of pastoral project in his first message to CELAM (Latin American Episcopal Conference) at a meeting in Rome in 1958, and again in 1961 when he sent an explicit request to all the episcopal conferences of the Latin American continent.

THE CONNECTION WITH THE COLLEGIALITY OF THE BISHOPS AND WITH THE EPISCOPAL CONFERENCES

In Europe comprehensive pastoral action developed in a diocese or a particular town. The pastoral projects, however, of Africa and Latin America mainly used the framework of the episcopal conferences. This was not the result of doctrinal attitudes but of concrete situations. The rapidity of social change and the weakness of diocesan organization in the developing countries called for common action on a higher level, often even before any more modest experiments had been launched. This was the case in Chile, the Congo (Leopoldville) and a large part of Brazil.

In Europe the episcopal conferences have been mainly concerned with coordination; and collegial action, in the full sense of the word, has been rare (as in the case of the Mission de France). The directives given by the Council may produce faster results, but they will no doubt be hampered by the heavy weight of existing Church organizations. This weight of institutionalism is felt less in developing countries, such as those mentioned above, and the means at the disposal of each bishop are far more limited. It has, therefore, been much easier there to link pastoral projects with decisions taken by the episcopal conference. However, since the field is still largely unexplored, there is still much difference both in the groundwork actually done and in the methods used.

For Latin America as a whole, little has been achieved. CELAM, which should normally have worked out these projects on the continental level, at least by directing aid coming from outside, has, in fact, done very little. One of the main reasons is that the Roman Curia had taken over this function through CAL (the Pontifical Commission for Latin America). Although it was decided at the end of the second session of the Council to reorganize it, CAL still leaves very little responsibility to the Latin Americans. Moreover, it does not even have the elementary means of working out a policy, and this is bound to lead to arbitrary action.

Insofar as the world at large is concerned, no attempt as yet has been made to integrate one or other activity into a comprehensive vision. It is enough to see how missionary activity has been conducted during the last decades. There is an almost total lack of the necessary knowledge (statistics, documentation and research) that might provide the foundation for such a vision on the level of the universal Church. It is to be hoped that the period after the Council will remedy this situation.

The Contents of Pastoral Organization

When we examine the contents of pastoral projects or the concrete shape of comprehensive pastoral work, we can see that it embraces all pastoral activity and usually leads to some precise measures according to the particular situation in which the Church is involved. It is, therefore, not enough to consider the initial launching of pastoral measures. This is pointed out in the previous reference on pastoral work in an industrial region:

Comprehensive pastoral work has often been described as a coordinating effort, a labor done in common, since "unity is strength". At the moment, our work is scattered from parish to parish and from one section of Christian and, particularly, secular action to another. We must put some

order into that anarchy, cut out overlapping activities and
see to it that everyone's action fully supports that of his
neighbor. Even though such a view of comprehensive pastoral work contains a grain of truth, it could also cause
complete stagnation in apostolic activity. It could lead to
mere organization of routine work, the coordination of
those organizations that do most damage to missionary
work, the concentration of pastoral initiative in the hands
of a few, the scientific organization of the ghetto and the
systematic erection of barricades. . . . No, comprehensive
pastoral work is not merely a question of organization. It
is, above all, a matter of discovering in common the evangelical needs of a region and the means to fill those needs.
It is not simply organization: it demands the renewal of the
contents. This is the direction in which we must go. The
socio-religious study of a region as a whole is the first important step in this direction. But it is only a step. The
gradual working out of a pastoral project—its realization
step-by-step, regular reexamination, all this accompanied by
the necessary reforms in organization—this is what comprehensive pastoral action means. Such pastoral activity is,
therefore, never finished, but always in progress.[2]

This leads us straight to a fundamental issue. This is not
merely concerned with an aspect of pastoral activity, or with
pastoral methods, or with a particular sphere of Church activity.
It concerns pastoral work itself. Hence, the need for a definition.
In most cases, unfortunately, it has been misunderstood. Both
comprehensive pastoral action and pastoral projects were first
undertaken by pastoral workers. If they had had to wait for
theologians to provide them with an adequate definition of their
work, they would probably never have started. It is, therefore,
hardly surprising that the theological substance of this work is
somewhat meager.

On the other hand, the wish to meet people of today in their

[2] L. Dingemans and F. Houtart, *op. cit.*, pp. 156-7.

concrete situation led pastoral workers to study the facts of social and religious life. It is this desire to work out details for such comprehensive pastoral activity and pastoral projects that produced many studies of varying importance in the field of religious sociology. We shall, therefore, have to consider the relations of these new forms of pastoral organization with theology on the one hand, and with sociology on the other.

Its Relation with Theology

Even when starting from an essentially empirical basis this pastoral renewal, as described above, required theology, at least implicitly. Such pastoral workers necessarily began with some conception of pastoral activity; otherwise, it would never have started at all. It was certainly broadly conceived and covered pastoral work as a whole. Everywhere, whether on the apostolic level or on that of secular activity, the integration of lay action was implied. In de-christianized regions particularly, the missionary idea dominated and there was a desire to create close links between organizations and persons who already had some missionary purpose, and those through whom the Christian community realizes itself, whether ritually or through personal contact.

Hence, the need to find a theological formula arose. By way of example, I quote the one given by Fr. Dingemans, O.P.: "Pastoral work is the activity by which the Church, moved by the Holy Spirit, visibly accomplishes the mission given her by Christ, and pursues the fulfillment of the Father's saving purpose with regard to the created world." [3] The author himself adds the comment that such a definition embraces all the activity of the Church without distinction of function (government, sacraments, teaching), nor of subject (faithful or unbelievers). It excludes, however, the pursuit of objectives that are in no way, or only very accidentally, connected with the proper mission of the Church.

But apart from a definition, which accounts for the all-

[3] L. Dingemans, "La Pastorale et ses buts généraux," in *Evangéliser* 17 (1962), n. 99, pp. 247ff.

embracing character of pastoral work, we still need constant theological reflection to deal with the various elements and their interrelation in comprehensive pastoral work. The parish, the role of the priest, the task of the laity in the secular field, the Church's attitude toward developing countries, etc.—all must be constantly accompanied by reflection. This thinking must not be speculative; it must be applied to the concrete facts of the region where comprehensive pastoral work is launched or a pastoral project is being worked out. Logically, it should follow the sociological work of which I shall speak later, but it is indispensable, and until now few theologians have devoted themselves to this task.

An interesting attempt has been made in this direction by a group of theologians and sociologists in Latin America, after the publication by FERES of important socio-religious research work covering the whole of that continent.[4] This group study has been published under the title, *The Tasks of the Church in Latin America*,[5] and deals first with the Church's attitude toward development there and then with the pastoral work involved. The two parts follow a similar plan: a brief survey of the basic facts, theological reflection on the problems raised, and then the application of this thinking to the Church's activity.

Its Relation with Sociology

It is not difficult to see that the sociological analysis of secular and religious phenomena is a basic condition for any rational pastoral organization. But here, too, there was much improvisation. Nobody is to blame. Pastoral workers felt the need for a renewal of pastoral activity based on empirical data. In Catholic circles sociology had not made much progress. In many places pastoral workers developed a sociology of their own.

At first, sociology was practically limited to statistics and surveys of religious activities. It was soon noticed that such methods

---

[4] Fédération internationale des Instituts de Recherches socio-religieuses (5, rue Guimard, Brussels 4).

[5] FERES, *Las tareas de la Iglesia en América Latina* (Fribourg, 1964).

were inadequate. Some studies by certain sociologists were perhaps not fully enough tuned in to pastoral activity and were too heavy both in substance and financially for the workers in this field. These misunderstandings are not yet all cleared up. There was even talk of a pastoral sociology that would have been sufficient to answer the needs of pastoral workers, and of a religious sociology of a more scientific character.

In fact, as in theology, we are faced with a twofold need. First, there is the need for research and basic studies on the various aspects of the relations between religion and society, on the organization of the Church and the various forms of its activity. Secondly, there is the need to apply whatever these studies reveal in the way of new ideas, possible work-schemes and up-to-date methods to the concrete needs of pastoral organization in each region. These two tasks are being undertaken by the institutes and centers of socio-religious research that exist at present in some twenty countries in Europe, America and Africa[6] and that form an international federation. The first type of work, however, tends to converge on the universities, while the second tends to be undertaken by ecclesiastical bodies such as the episcopal conferences, conferences of religious congregations, dioceses, etc.

EXAMPLES OF COMPREHENSIVE PASTORAL WORK AND PASTORAL PROJECTS

Before tackling the question of the methods and bodies that deal with these two aspects, we might have a look at what is being done at the moment.

1. *Comprehensive Pastoral Work*

Most of the experiments in this field are being made in France. Influenced by the work of Canon Boulard, about forty French dioceses have begun to organize both a decentralization based on "human zones" and the integration of all fields of apostolic

[6] See article on contribution made by sociology to pastoral work, p. 89.

activity. This comprehensive approach takes place on both the local and the diocesan level. Among the more important dioceses that of Lyons stands out as being the most advanced. This diocese has not only been divided into several zones, including the urban ones of Lyons and St-Etienne, but new divisions have been created within each zone. In Lyons there are three levels, based on geographical redistribution: the parish, the deanery and the "sector". The deanery brings together the parochial clergy and ensures their organic collaboration. The "sector" usually links two deaneries according to the geographical layout of the town. Here is where the various specialized forms of apostolate, such as specialized Catholic Action, teaching, hospitals, religious congregations, etc., are first brought together with the parochial apostolate.

Each level has its own responsible leader: the parish priest, the dean, the sector leader and the leader of the zone. There are specialized commissions for the zone and for the sectors. One of the most effective means of integration lies in the fact that practically every parish priest has some special responsibility that goes beyond his parochial territory. Such an organization of pastoral work offers at least the best chance of seeing the problems of evangelization as a whole, of avoiding the danger of concentrating on Church organizations and forgetting the people.

For some years already, the town of Rotterdam, too, has recreated its pastoral organization as a result of a study made by the Katholiek Sociaal Kerkelijk Instituut (KSKI). Here the deanery is the basic unit, while the town has been divided into sectors according to some activity done in common.

The Latin American experiment in comprehensive pastoral work was the first to receive canonical recognition. Since 1958 the southern parishes of Bogotá, mainly proletarian quarters, have formed an association, later recognized as a *pia unio,* and linking more than thirty parishes in one organic activity. When this association started, there were only about a dozen parishes. The main question was the organization of food distribution to people who were starving and who had streamed into the town partly because of the violence that had broken out in certain districts of the country.

The collaboration, therefore, started as a charitable activity, but it quickly spread to education, liturgy, catechetics, specialized Catholic Action, etc. This comprehensive activity functions through two organs: the general assembly of the parish priests (most parishes have only one priest) and an executive committee chosen by the parish priests. There are also a number of specialized commissions on which the bishop is represented by a parish priest whom he has delegated for this. It is interesting to note that among the parochial leaders there are not only priests of the diocese but also religious from more than ten different congregations. In France, Canon Boulard organizes regular meetings of leaders from dioceses where this comprehensive pastoral work has been going on so that they can share their experiences, successes and failures.

2. Pastoral Projects

The first pastoral projects on a national level were launched at the same time, in 1961, in Chile and in the Congo (Leopoldville). The Brazilian project followed in 1962. We shall deal with these three countries, and make mention of some other similar efforts.

In the case of the first two, a sociological study together with a theological examination provided the groundwork. The Chilean project was based on similar work done by FERES since 1958. In the Congo the work continued the preliminary efforts made since 1959 by a center of socio-religious research. Certain parts of this work had already been done before that date.

The projects were worked out in Chile, the first in 1961, the second toward the end of 1963.[7] A group of theologians and sociologists met for several months and put in thirty full working days of collaboration. They started from the social and religious situation and worked out the principal objectives for apostolic

[7] "Plan pastoral de l'Episcopat chilien," in *Bulletin d'information de Pro Mundi Vita* (Tilburg, 1964).

activity in Chile. They decided, for example, on the organization of a general mission covering the whole country. This mission was to be based on the preaching of the Word rather than on laboring sacramental practice. One of the principal aims was to put new life into the spirit and methods of pastoral work. Another aim was to make better use of mass media, particularly by preparing radio programs to be sent out by already existing transmitters. A third aim was to strengthen apostolic activity in State education, especially among its professors and teachers.

The document prepared by the bishops also envisaged the various executive bodies: episcopal commissions, specialized services such as centers for liturgy, catechetics, social and religious research, etc., and a technical service for pastoral planning.

In the Congo political events obviously forced the Church to reconsider her situation and her pastoral activity in that society.[8] The document starts with a sociological appreciation of the Church's situation: its relations with the Government, supplementary activity in such fields as health and education, the too faithful copying of the kind of apostolate that prevailed in Belgium, etc. The second part deals with the doctrinal aspects of the present situation: the relations between Church and State, the Church and education, the Church and the temporal factors, the role played by the laity, etc. The third part is devoted to concrete suggestions.

Envisaging the end of Christian dominance, the document gives some indications about the role of Christian organizations: temporary and short-term replacement. One chapter deals with the basic units of this society and their organization. Mention is also made of the role to be played by religious (male and female) and catechists. It ends with a reminder of the importance of comprehensive pastoral work in the words of Pope Pius XII: "It is as wrong to believe that only pastoral organization on the human level can guarantee the progress of Christianity as it is to pretend that free growth and whole spontaneous organization

[8] *Actes de la VIe Assemblée plenière de l'Episcopat du Congo* (Leopoldville, 1961).

of apostolic activity can do so" (To Lenten preachers, 1955).

Locally, the project suggests three elements: the team of priests that links the priests of a locality, the apostolic team that includes other religious cooperators, and the parochial team that incorporates the laity. The problem is studied in detail for the situation in town and rural areas. It is suggested that in rural areas every mission be divided into a number of sectors that would each link together several villages and with a central branch office in one of these. The missions would keep their specialized teamwork. In the towns, deaneries would be organized to form the first link for interparochial pastoral work. On the diocesan level five specialized teams would be organized to deal with urban apostolate, rural apostolate, pastoral work in secondary education, liturgical work and youth.

Lastly, on the national level the bishops would make a determined effort to coordinate the available information, the rationalized use of resources and vocations and the organization of socio-religious research work.

As far as Brazil is concerned,[9] the emergency project worked out in 1962 began also by facing the facts. Perhaps because it was worked out more quickly than the two previous ones, the analysis turned out to be less thorough. Since the project covered a vast country and was, therefore, conceived in much more general terms, the great directives tended to be more theoretical. It was decided to divide Brazil into seven regions (today eleven) that would group the bishops into regional conferences. Each region was then invited to work out its own pastoral project.

There were three main points in this first general project: the need for comprehensive action, the encouragement of lay activity and a change in the mentality of Catholic education. The results were most encouraging. Regional conferences met and a certain number of them worked out projects in great detail, including even definite timing and a budget. Much of this effort owes its success to the Movement for a Better World.

[9] *Plano da Emergencia. Conf. dos Bispos do Brasil* (Rio de Janeiro, 1962).

The region where this planning action originated was the northeast, and particularly the diocese of Natal.[10] Under the active guidance of Archbishop Eugenio Sales of Natal, yearly projects had been worked out in the diocese for some time and the method was gradually extended to the whole region. In the diocese of Natal, too, the territory was divided into zones: the town of Natal and five rural zones. The project dealt with each of these six units, and also with action on the level of the diocese as a whole. Every important sector of specialized activity was also provided with a monthly program.

In the project of 1963, for instance, dealing with the diocesan sector of secondary education, the first three months had to be given up to a survey of the situation in the diocese. Then a provincial Secretariat for Catholic education was set up, and this was followed by a study of the new ideas contained in the general project accepted by all the bishops of Brazil. After that, meetings with members of the teaching profession were to be organized. And lastly, a scheme was to be worked out for the spiritual and apostolic reform of each individual establishment. For the following months other activities were laid down: courses for the formation of student leaders, societies for fathers, etc.

Several other dioceses of Latin America have planned pastoral projects, such as Riobamba in Ecuador, which has done this since 1958. On the other hand, in the African countries of Burundi and Rwanda, the bishops have made their project a five-year plan for 1964-1968,[11] but this is of another kind. It tries to assess the future needs of the Church, particularly in matters of organization, in view of the demographic, social and economic evolution of the two countries. The document contains a brief analysis of the existing situation, concentrating on personnel and organizations. It then proceeds to plan what will be required year by year and to budget for each step forward.

It is clear that the projects differ considerably in contents.

[10] *Pastoral de Conjunto* (Arquid. de Natal, 1964).
[11] *Burundi et Rwanda 1964-1968. Plan quinquennal de développement.* (Usumbura, Conférence des Ordinaires du Rwanda et du Burundi, 1963).

The methods used, too, vary and are not always satisfactory from the technical point of view. Nevertheless, all these efforts have one basic point in common: they all represent an attempt at rationalizing pastoral activity, which up till now was mainly conspicuous for a somewhat unbridled improvisation.

3. The Methods

The methods for working out a comprehensive pastoral policy and pastoral projects have much in common. It is, of course, important to emphasize the primacy of the pastoral purpose in all this. Yet, it must also be pointed out clearly that a certain technique must be followed. It would appear that five stages are indispensable, and if, in the examples mentioned above, they have not always been followed, the need for them was nevertheless sharply underlined:

(a) Knowledge of the world to be evangelized, and of the concrete relationship between the Church and this world; this is the socio-religious stage.

(b) Theological reflection on the Church's mission in this concrete world.

(c) When the previous two steps have brought out the main points for the direction in which this pastoral work should be deployed, a program of evangelization should be drafted accordingly.

(d) A project of evangelization should then be worked out, setting out in detail the stages by which it should proceed and the way in which responsibility should be distributed.

(e) There must be a regular revision of the project.

Each of these stages has its own methods and there is no need to go into details here. Unfortunately, very often these methods are not taken seriously. Many failures can be attributed mainly to a certain contempt for the technique at one stage or another, without mentioning the lack of experience for which there is an excuse at least.

Yet, there are certain aspects of this task that I would like to develop a little: first of all, the working out of the pastoral project. Some documents leave one with the impression that they have been worked out in one or other episcopal curia without taking account of the practical possibilities. Others call "project" what is in fact only a general program, without such necessary details as selection, assessment of priorities, timing, precise definition of the various responsibilities, and so on. Lastly, a fair amount of initial decisions have been taken without bringing in the people on the ground floor. The result has been that priests feel they are there only to carry out decisions taken at the top, and that they have had no say in these matters. This inevitably creates the wrong kind of atmosphere and hinders the smooth execution of the project. One of the basic requirements of development and communal organization is that the workers on the ground floor are associated with the project at all stages. If, therefore, the clergy and laity have not been allowed to share in the preparation of this pastoral renewal, there will be little chance of their joining spontaneously in its execution.

All this obviously presupposes a new training, especially in the case of the clergy and religious. This is why practically all that has been done in this domain has been accompanied by a corresponding advance in training. This includes courses in pastoral training, institutes of pastoral activity and even a reform of the seminaries, as in the diocese of Mechlin-Brussels. In this direction the greatest advance has probably been made in Latin America. In the northeast province of Brazil, for instance, there are even courses for the bishops. Again, in Mexico this renewal has been launched by some twenty dioceses working together according to a detailed plan that starts with courses for the clergy organized by the Latin American Institute of Pastoral Activity.

4. The Bodies

Certain bodies have proved to be necessary. For instance, wherever the extent of the zone or diocese did not allow the bishop to lead this comprehensive pastoral work himself, a special leader has been appointed. Almost everywhere, too, there was an obvious need to set up a Secretariat for this work. This same pastoral development also calls for certain specialized services, such as catechetical centers, centers for the liturgy, etc., that inevitably require a degree of specialization and, therefore, complementary activity on the part of the clergy. All this leads to a certain bureaucratic (in the technical sense of the word) organization of pastoral work, which often creates conflicts with the already existing ecclesiastical bureaucracy that until now has been mainly administrative. We shall gradually have to integrate these two aspects.

Lastly, insofar as some thinking has to be done, centers of socio-religious research and teams of theologians are indispensable. Apart from certain rare exceptions, however, all this can hardly be provided by each diocese. Cooperation will, therefore, be necessary between dioceses, between episcopal conferences and between the conferences of religious congregations.

In this field, the Dutch hierarchy has made a significant move. They have set up a Pastoral Institute (Pastoraal Instituut van de Nederlandse Kerkprovincie), devoted to study, and not to teaching. Its task is to prepare the ground for pastoral decisions, on the basis of advice given by about one hundred clerical and lay experts, theologians and the members of the Institute for socio-religious research (KSKI). Actually, its task is to advise bishops and major superiors on pastoral matters in the widest sense of that word and to make the necessary contacts. It also looks after the necessary liaison between the higher religious authorities, the clergy and the faithful, and between the various movements and organizations engaged in apostolic work. This Institute was set up in 1963.

Conclusions

Comprehensive pastoral activity and pastoral projects correspond to several basic tendencies that prevail in both the world and the Church today. From the sociological point of view they correspond to the great movement of rationalization that pervades all sectors of man's collective existence and which *Mater et Magistra* called "socialization". It is the fruit of specialization in the field of man's social activities and of the increasingly varied and powerful means of communication. If we define pastoral work sociologically as the "communication" of a message of life, it is normal that the human methods used for this communication should be adapted to the society in which we live, according to the Lord's wish that we should cooperate. This in no way diminishes the eminently personal character of this message. It is precisely to establish a personal contact with a greater number of persons that it is necessary to use adequate means of communication.

From the apostolic point of view, this movement of thought and action corresponds to the new needs of modern evangelization: regions or social sectors that have become completely dechristianized, pastoral work in regions that are subject to rapid social changes, completely new conditions that prevail in the mission field.

No doubt, only time will tell whether these pastoral methods are adequate. I have simply tried to show what is involved, that they presuppose a profound reassessment of all pastoral activity, based on socio-religious research and theological reflection, and how they imply a new training of all those who have a specific pastoral task to perform.

Jan Kerkhofs, S.J./ *Heverlee, Belgium*

Church Aid for
Developing Countries

INTRODUCTORY REMARKS:
WHAT IS CHURCH AID FOR DEVELOPING COUNTRIES?

Modern action aiming at the realization of justice and love on an international level varies and changes with baffling rapidity. Any definition of Church aid in this sense can only be tentative and provisional. The concept of the Church and the theology of earthly realities are still in the process of growth, and theories about aid to developing countries germinate. As a workable hypothesis one might say that this aid covers any social and economic effort, individual or collective, that aims at helping certain regions of the world, with living standards far below the level achieved in Western Europe and America, to become equal partners in the use and creation of material and cultural prosperity in a world that becomes increasingly one.[1] Such aid, moreover, implies that the assistance given does not cause any basic

---

* JAN KERKHOFS, S.J.: Born May 19, 1924 in Hasselt, Limbourg, Belgium, he became a Jesuit and was ordained in 1956. He studied at the Jesuit Faculty in Louvain, the University of Louvain and Oxford University, earning his doctorate in sociology in 1954. He is professor of moral and pastoral theology in the Jesuit Faculty at Louvain, professor of pastoral sociology at the Institut supérieur de Sciences religieuses of the University of Louvain, professor of sociology at the University of Antwerp and national spiritual director of Patrons catholiques flamands.

[1] *Encyclique "Mater et Magistra," Commentaire par l'Action Populaire* (Paris, 1962), p. 147.

43

disturbance in the cultural individuality of these economically
backward countries, but rather encourages them to find new
ways of self-expression.[2] This aid can be given in countless different ways, ranging from purely private initiative to collective
action by groups of nations or by the United Nations as a whole.
As this aid must always imply a growth toward equality, it must
equally imply the cooperation and co-responsibility of the developing countries.

Church aid in the strict sense is aid that is provided by Christians as such and, in one way or other, collectively. This excludes help given by the individual Christian without any link
to the Christian community as such. It is not always easy to draw
the line between Church aid and Christian aid in general without this link, just as it is difficult to distinguish between *actio
catholica* and *actio catholicorum*. Church aid is, for instance, the
aid given by missionary orders and congregations, or by the
various Lenten actions in Western Europe, or by the NCWC and
similar organizations, or by groups of lay technologists when
presented as explicitly Christian, or the social, economic, medical
or cultural contributions made under the auspices of the local
hierarchy or of Catholic organizations, where these assist the
country's own development, etc.

This definition provokes numerous questions: How far must
the Church go, in providing this aid? Is it not enough for in-
dividual Christians to become integrated in organizations that
already exist for this purpose? If not, how does disinterested
Church aid fit in with apostolic activity? How far can a local
Church community have some real say in the form and application of contributions, human or material, sent by their country?
What criteria can ensure that the help is justified from both the
Christian point of view and from that of actual needs? How can
Church aid (*e.g.,* when linked with government support) escape
even the appearance of neo-colonialism? How should the laity
of both the aiding and the aided countries share in the responsi-

[2] *Ibid.,* p. 157; *Encyclique "Pacem in Terris," Commentaire par l'Action populaire* (Paris, 1963), p. 125.

bility—a particularly important point since most of this question falls in the realm of the temporal.[3]

These questions make it clear that Church aid is a very complex reality that involves religious loyalty, the need for apostolic planning, the Christian concept of the profane, the layman's share in ecclesiastical decisions. It is a new aspect of the wider question concerning the visible incarnation of the Church as such and the responsible realization of this incarnation. One could conceive this problem as the dialectics of power and service. On the one hand, the Church as Church must manifest itself as the servant of humanity during the pilgrimage of the whole creation to the kingdom of God. On the other hand, the conviction of Christians who remain human, with all the implications of that word, deliberately seeks incarnation; this assumes influence, often power, frequently political power.[4]

There are two rather extreme simplifications that might lift the tension between service and power: the first is to withdraw into a kind of apostolic nihilism that makes us ineffectual and futile both as Christians and as human beings under the pretext of a theoretical goodwill and humility; the second is to lead power away from service and to misuse it for denominational politics by not understanding the apostolic law of death and resurrection, and out of human weakness. These considerations,

[3] *Welvaart, Welzijn en Geluk. Een katholiek uitzicht op de Nederlandse samenleving,* part V (Hilversum-Antwerp, 1963), pp. 270ff. This deals with the problem of State subsidy for the missions. In Germany (more than 100 million DM for Catholic and Protestant development projects) and in Switzerland (2.8 million Swiss FR for Church-aid projects during the period 1962-1964), the State subsidizes the missions. In the Netherlands the question is under discussion. In Belgium there is rather a negative attitude, also on the Church's side, toward State aid for the missions; here the indirect support given within the framework of general regulations for technical volunteers is preferred.

[4] The danger is not wholly imaginary that the Church's certain overemphasis of the poor might lead to the same kind of extreme as the flight from the "flesh" brought about in the attitude toward marriage: political power is suspect because of its ambiguity. Nevertheless, power is an earthly reality that can and must be christianized as much as sexuality. It is in no case a negative value or a kind of "no man's land" insofar as Christian morality is concerned.

together with what follows, are only intended as a small contribution to deeper study of a problem about which there exists little technical literature.

I

WHY CHURCH AID?

Perhaps the least incorrect answer to this question is that the Church has always provided this aid *avant la lettre*. Throughout the Church's history, from the institution of the diaconate, the care of the poor, the *monte di pietá*, the Jesuit organization of Paraguay, the schools of the Brethren of the Common Life, up to contemporary Christian action, *caritas catholica* and catholic education, the Church has tried to help those who fell behind in one way or other. However imperfect its methods were, the Church always provided this aid as Church, *i.e.*, as a group that tried to apply the faith in concrete activity, and so to render a modern version of the parable of the good Samaritan and of the 25th chapter of St. Matthew. Most Protestant Churches have remained faithful to this pre-Reformation tradition, and they, too, collectively manifested their wish to serve in all kinds of activities.

Aid by the Church as an Institution

Is it really necessary that Church aid be institutionalized? Would it not be better if, as (so often quite correctly) classical forms of Christian aid were secularized (*e.g.*, social welfare), the whole of this aid were detached from the Churches and given on a strictly neutral basis and on international, multilateral lines? This question, applied to the situation of developing countries, concerns the meaning of confessional or, more broadly, ideological structures outside the strictly religious sphere. Although the study of this crucial problem is beyond the scope of this article, it cannot be entirely ignored here.

First of all, there is a distinction between strictly confessional and ideologically inspired structures. Where Christians in general, or Catholics in particular, are sufficiently numerous to have their own schools, hospitals, youth work, etc., they are entitled to these, also in developing countries, on the ground of freedom of association, although this implies by no means that it is pastorally opportune.

Where, however, they are in a small minority, or where the presence of these good works might hamper the normal freedom of belief because of the material advantages they offer, it would appear preferable to have organizations, either not explicitly Christian even though based on Christian principles or, as the case may be, exclusively based on natural rights. Moreover, this holds just as much for developed countries and predominantly Catholic ones. In principle this means that in certain circumstances and for certain sectors such as education, medical help and social action, the work will be done more efficiently, both on the Christian level and on that of universal humanity, if Protestants and Catholics, or more broadly, Christians and other believers such as Muhammadans work together.

But in many developing countries the problem is in fact quite different: there it concerns the choice between a pluralistic system and a severely uniform and centralized State system where, in many cases, either Communism, or an undefined State Socialism, or a single recognized religion (Islam, Buddhism) provides an ideological trend.

Even in the case mentioned above, where the Church can provide aid by means of her own institutions, it does not follow that every form of explicitly ecclesiastical institution is opportune. One may well ask whether it would not be better if a group of organized Christians (*e.g.*, educators and teachers) were integrated in international organizations for neutral help or in the national organizations of a State, and did their work rather by means of penetration than by means of institutionalized organizations of their own confession or ideology.[5]

[5] The problem of denominationalism in developing countries has been dealt with in many pastoral letters. Cf. "Le chrétien dans la cité" (Pastoral Letter of the Bishops of Haute-Volta, Jan. 27, 1959), in *Documentation Catholique* (1959), col. 541ff.; "Les Problèmes posés par une société

In my opinion, there is no universally valid solution for this problem. On the one hand, the faithful, also as a community, must be able to give effective expression to their ideology (at least insofar as basic natural principles are concerned) in order to ensure a minimum of social "witness"; on the other hand, neither in the young nations nor in the old Atlantic States should this community become a State religion or withdraw into a ghetto, an alien element in the healthy progress of a nation.

It is normal that there will be tensions between the pluralist point of view and that of a centralizing State. As recent history has shown, it is even possible that no compromise can be found workable, as when political power is either totally corrupt or indulges in extreme Marxism and extreme liberalism. This usually leads to persecution of Christians as well as the whole people.

Should This Aid Be "Disinterested" or Tend toward Evangelization?

At a meeting on Voluntary Service Overseas, Prof. A. Dondeyne of Louvain posed this question: "How can cooperation for development be justified in the light of faith and the Christian conscience, if it aims exclusively at this development in itself and remains uninfluenced by any economic, political or religious self-interest?" [6] The answer to this apparent dilemma is that Church aid, too, accepts both types of aid, in theory as well as in practice, as shown by the action of MISEREOR,[6a] which makes financial contributions to the FAO, or by Catholic technologists, put at the disposal of foreign States by Christian institutions. It seems meaningless to try to establish some priority of one of the two types over the other: some will be more in-

---

pluraliste" (Pastoral Letter of the Bishops of Tanganyika), in *Documentation Catholique* (1961), col. 1297-1306; *Lettre pastorale des vicaries et préfets apostoliques du Congo Belge et du Ruanda-Burundi*, Aug. 22, 1959 (Leopoldstad-Brussels, 1959); see also Cardinal Liénart's address "Le Concile—les institutions chrétiennes," in *Documentation Catholique* (1964), col. 767-8.

[6] A. Dondeyne, "De ontwikkelingshulp in christelijk perspectief," in *De Gids op Maatschappelijk Gebied* 53 (Brussels, 1964), p. 189.

[6a] The German Bishops' Campaign against Hunger and Disease.

clined personally to help out of Christian motives of justice or the wish to serve without any explicitly apostolic motive, while others will provide the same help as an explicit witness to their faith, without excluding justice and brotherly love. The final theological justification of "disinterested" aid is the same as the one that gives a Christian sense to any commitment on the secular level. The attitude of basic commitment to the will of the creator implies for the Christian that he collaborate in perfecting creation on every level of human existence. In the present perspective of universal redemption, any such cooperation is already in itself Christian without requiring the addition of an explicitly apostolic aspect (see Matt. 25).

On the other hand, aid tending toward evangelization is no less "disinterested" than so-called un-ideological aid. Apart from the explicitly confessional character of actions done in faith, all human activity is basically ideological. This ideology, particularly when given some social expression, adds its own characteristics to the society it influences. In contrast, a spiritual choice, which cannot express itself outwardly, remains incomplete. The co-existence of several spiritual choices embodied in society is the very definition of a pluralistic community. With this is connected the fact that collective help, particularly of the lasting kind, will in most cases show some ideological traces.

Convinced ideologists believe in their choice and in the main features of their image of society. They want to share this with others because they are convinced that this is the right conception, even for the developing country, and because they consider that the universal realization of their concept of society is important for the international interdependence of all States. That is why precisely the two most powerful ideologies, Christianity and Marxism, are most concerned with aid based on a definite view of the world, and the absence of such a concept constitutes precisely the basic weakness in the massive aid activities of the United States.[7]

[7] Miss Barbara Ward, a former editor of *The Economist,* wrote justly: "The lack of any political or ideological framework is the greatest single source of weakness in the aid programme undertaken by the West."

II

THE CHANNELS OF CHURCH AID

Here again, we leave aside individual Christian help, however important as in FAO, WHO, UNESCO, and limit the discussion to what is strictly Church aid. There are three main channels for dispensing this aid. The first channel is to influence public opinion in both the developing and the developed countries. This is done through papal encyclicals, pastoral letters,[8] through propaganda in scientific[9] and popular periodicals and through the formation of the right mentality in special departments at Catholic universities, in television, in courses by radio, etc. The second channel is that of financial help. The actions for Lent and Advent launched by the bishops of Western Europe, and the various Freedom from Hunger campaigns are a modern expression of the Church's preoccupations in this field. The impressive organization of these activities and the fact that the national hierarchies administer the financial contributions collectively help to explain their exceptional success. Finally, and most important of all, there is the personal commitment of tens of thousands of Catholics who, collectively and supported by the Church, serve both man and God in the furtherance of this development. Indeed, the aid provided by orders, congregations and lay organizations constitutes a most important asset of capital and knowledge that, because of its durability and long experience, is more effective than most official organizations.[10]

[8] See, among others, A. J. Fougerat, Bishop of Grenoble, "De internationale plicht van katholieken," in *Katholiek Archief* 16 (1961), col. 1037-46 and the statement by the Bishops' Conference of CELAM (Spanish text in *Ecclesia* [Dec. 5, 1959]; French text in *Doc. Cath.* 57 [1960], col. 169-74). Cf. also Archbishop J. C. Heenan, "A Call to Action," in Arthur McCormack, *Christian Responsibility and World Poverty; A Catholic Viewpoint* (London, 1963), pp. 293-9, and the Pastoral Letter of the American Bishops: "The World 'Population Explosion'," in *Catholic Mind* (March-April, 1960), pp. 185-8.

[9] E. g., *Justice dans le Monde (World Justice)*, University of Louvain.

[10] Dr. Oskar Splett, "Entwicklungshilfe in ihren menchlichen Zielen," in Robert Siegert, *Entwicklungshilfe-einmal anders. Schriftenreihe zum Handbuch der Entwicklungshilfe* (Heft 10, Baden-Baden/Bonn, 1963), pp. 129ff.

Here some key questions about the application of Church aid must be mentioned.

Relationship between Church Aid and Other Aid

In Church aid, strictly so called, assistance and apostolic witness coincide. It is aimed at the whole man, *i.e.*, at man on his way to God. Official bilateral or multilateral aid and the assistance given by various development organizations are directed toward the improvement of social and economic conditions. Both channels of aid may well, in fact, work out the same kind of project, such as community development, foundation of hospitals, education, etc.; yet the spirit remains different. Church aid is necessarily and always a possible approach toward the faith, although this will mainly be by the creation of living conditions that are more favorable to the free acceptance of the faith.

However, this difference of spiritual level does not deny that strict Church aid should integrate itself in the whole development policy of a given country. This coordination of Church aid with other aid is, moreover, a necessary condition for apostolic witness: unless aid is genuine and effective it cannot make genuine spiritual witness shine through it. This demands a constant dialogue with other development bodies and particularly with the State itself on the organizational level. It is here that the function of the national episcopal conferences becomes indispensable in both the giving and receiving countries.[11] On the other hand, religious orders and congregations provide the largest contingent of Church helpers, while the laity provide a constantly increasing number of temporary or permanent technological volunteers. As a result the hierarchy must be assisted in the dialogue by a body —whatever its constitution—composed of delegates from the national federations of the higher superiors, men and women, and of lay people sharing in both advice and decisions. With the help

[11] Those who assist must avoid any kind of neo-colonialism. See Mario von Galli, "Der Christ und die Entwicklungshilfe," in *Zeichen unter den Völkern* (Mainz, 1962), pp. 113ff.

of a service for technical advice, this body should represent Church aid wherever it comes into contact with the other forms of aid.

It is obvious that national coordination will not suffice. Aiding countries do not act bilaterally: religious congregations and the great lay organizations are international and send international teams to numerous countries. Even among the Lenten actions, contacts develop from year to year by which certain projects can be financed in combination and overlapping can be avoided. The developing countries can only profit by coordination in order to make planning for aid both possible and sound. The example of Latin America shows this: the episcopal conference of CELAM and the federation of national associations of higher superiors, CLAR, grew out of the need for common efforts to deal with common problems.[12] Thanks to this kind of organization—and to the excellent studies brought out by such technical advice services as DESAL,[13] set up by MISEREOR and other movements in order to establish a list of priorities—it becomes possible to arrive gradually at some form of planning that is as necessary as it is delicate. The need for this kind of institutionalization is also increasingly felt in Africa. This will slowly lead to a coordination based on continents or subcontinents rather than on individual nations.

In this context, mention must be made of the new organization, *Pro Mundi Vita*. There is indeed an urgent and constant need for a center of international contact that transmits information concerning needs and opportunities for assistance, particularly of a pastoral nature. *Pro Mundi Vita* should be considered as an attempt to serve in this way all those who are responsible in the Church and to allow them to make pastoral decisions

---

[12] F. Houtart, "Les formes modernes de collégialité épiscopale," in *L'Episcopat et l'Eglise Universelle* (*Unam Sanctam* 39, Paris, 1962), pp. 497-535.

[13] Centro para el desarollo economico y social de America Latina, with headquarters in Santiago, Chile, founded in order to make the contributions by *Misereor, Adveniat, Oostpriesterhulp,* etc., as effective as possible.

based on exact information provided on the lines of supply and demand.[14]

Gradually the national and international episcopal commissions as well as the centers of assistance and information will have to coordinate Church aid with two other forms of assistance in development, *viz.*, Protestant Church aid and those development organizations not specifically representative of a Church but nevertheless based on Christian foundations. As examples of this latter category ICV (International Federation of Christian Trade Unions) and UNIAPAC (International Federation of Christian Employers and Managers) might be mentioned. The hierarchy should not force these organizations to take on tasks that explicitly belong to Church aid, since these organizations are not exclusively Catholic but admit all groups of a personalist character. In practice, too, they must be left the necessary freedom of action. The same holds for the relations between Church aid and the aid provided by groups of lay Christians who devote themselves to this kind of assistance without an explicitly Christian label. There is no point in integrating them into official ecclesiastical organizations. The words of Scripture apply here: "He who is not against you is for you" (Mark 9, 39). But the hierarchy will have to watch that there is no overlapping with these minor or major enterprises.

Relation between Church Aid and the Laity

The danger of exporting Western European clericalism to the developing countries precisely through this Church aid is not imaginary. Even more than in the countries of early Christendom their priests and religious are social leaders and technical experts involved in heavy responsibilities concerned with the secular side of life.[15] The importance of teams composed of priests, religious

[14] *La Responsabilité universelle des Chrétiens,* report of the PMV Congress of 1964, Brussels. PMV's headquarters are at Brussels.
[15] This is not a "necessary evil". N. Drogat, *Pays sous-développés et coopération technique* (Bibl. de la recherche sociale, Paris, 1959), quotes article VII of the important convention signed in December 1957 at La

54   JAN KERKHOFS, S.J.

and the laity can hardly be overrated.[16] With a few exceptions, not much progress has been made on this point because even in Europe and America the turning point has only recently been reached. The training, both before and after ordination or profession, of priests and religious (indigenous and foreign) in the developed countries will have to pay more serious attention to this need for a genuine dialogue with the laity. Not only a sound theology of the Church but also straightforward, sound, practical reasons urgently demand this cooperation with the laity. In many developing countries "adult" missionary institutions are nationalized, particularly in education and medicine; this often means that explicitly ecclesiastical responsibilities are excluded. The spiritual orientation of such secularized institutions can, then, only be provided by responsible lay people.[17]

Specific Opportunities of Church Aid

As has been rightly pointed out, the disappointments experienced in the massive assistance given officially by the West during the last ten years has caused much talk of a crisis, if not failure.[18] Material assistance, without the personal assistance required to integrate it mentally and orally, has led in many places to social chaos and the moral bankruptcy of whole societies. In

---

Paz between the Holy See and the Government of Bolivia in favor of the Catholic missions among the native population: "Along with the evangelization of the natives, which constitutes the first end of their apostolate, the missionaries will concern themselves with the material prosperity of the territory and its inhabitants. To this end, each Vicar Apostolic will study and will have studied, calling upon appropriate techniques, the industrial and commercial possibilities of his territory. He will communicate the result of his investigations to the supreme government which will give to the Vicars Apostolic the necessary aid for the development of agriculture and the industries that can be established, as well as for the establishment of cooperatives and social works" (p. 30).

[16] *Local Leadership in Mission Lands. Proceedings of the Fordham University Conference of Mission Specialists* (New York, 1954).

[17] M. Ducos, O. P., *Pour un apostolat organisé* (Coll. Recherches Pastorales, Paris, 1963), pp. 176ff.

[18] W. Buehlmann, "Entwicklungshilfe und Mission," in *Katholisches Missionsjahrbuch der Schweiz/Annuaire missionnaire catholique de la Suisse* (1963), pp. 6-19; F. A. Plattner, "Der Bundesrat spricht zur Entwicklungshilfe," in *Orientierung* 28 (1964), pp. 151-4.

contrast, modest Church aid has exceptional opportunities here precisely because it invests in personal, long-term and complete integration in the people who receive this assistance. The many thousands of small projects carried out by missionaries and lay-helpers throughout the world, supported by the Christian organizations on both sides of the Atlantic, surpass all official assistance in actual effectiveness. Here, appropriate projects have been realized with accelerating effect, in cooperation with those most concerned, and with a constant eye on the overall development of the whole community. It would also appear that the faith alone often gives the strength to persevere with assistance and encouragement in spite of disappointment and misunderstanding.

Church aid is perhaps the most appropriate way to express in concrete fashion the universality of the Church in an increasingly unified world. The message conveyed through this aid will be tested by the genuineness of this universality. That is why the key question in Church aid seems to be that of motive: for many people in the developing countries it is not yet clear whether the Church wants to serve or to rule; whether she truly identifies herself with the people or whether she still clings, however covertly, to a kind of foreign paternalism.[19] On this point, the bishops of both developed and developing countries should take up a clear position, repeatedly and collectively, and so reinforce the definite statements given by Pope John XXIII in his two great encyclicals. This clear position should be publicized by press and radio and should become as much public knowledge in the developing countries as Communist propaganda from Moscow or Peking. A wrong interpretation of the meaning and tendency of Church aid could easily boomerang with deadly results for the apostolate and, as in China, close the door for many years. This leads to a new problem, the problem of Christian effectiveness, but its treatment would require a separate article.

[19] Ph. Laurent, "Vision chrétienne du développement économique," in *Revue de l'Action Populaire* (Paris, Nov. 1961), pp. 1043-60; L. Grond, F. Houtart and C. Thoen, "De Kerk en de hulp aan de ontwikkelingslanden. Voorwaarden tot doeltreffende actie," in *Katholiek Archief* 17 (1962), pp. 289-312.

Aloysius Fonseca, S.J. / *Bombay, India*

Pastoral Experience and Perspectives in India

No pastoral policy to be effective can be framed in a vacuum. It must be fashioned to secure its objectives in a particular set of circumstances at a particular period of time. This is all the more necessary in an ancient society that is undergoing a series of rapid changes. India is an old country with a civilization encrusted in a social structure that has stood the strain of centuries, but is now breaking down under the pressures of an expanding industrial and technological invasion. The impact of the machine on India's traditional way of life has been gradual up to now, but the process has been greatly accelerated by the conscious efforts to industrialize the country after independence. The new rulers of India are convinced that India must catch up with the developed countries of the West, and believe that only a rapid rate of technological

* ALOYSIUS FONSECA, S.J.: Born January 16, 1915 in Karachi, India, he became a Jesuit and was ordained in 1948. He studied at St. Joseph's College in Trichinopoly, the Gregorian University in Rome and the Economische Hogeschool at Tilburg, earning his doctorate in economics at Tilburg in 1960 with the thesis, "Wage Determination and Organized Labour in India". He conducts courses in trade unionism at St. Xavier's College, Bombay, teaches social ethics at St. Pius X Seminary in Bombay, lectures on industrial relations at Loyola College, Madras and at St. Xavier's College, Ranchi, and is editor of *Social Action*. He has written many articles on labor economics, and has contributed to a number of periodicals including *Civiltà Cattolica* (Rome), *Economic Weekly* (India), *Examiner* (India) and the *Indian Journal of Social Work*.

progress can ensure to the country the material advantages enjoyed by the inhabitants of Europe and North America.

In this drive toward an industrial society, a social upheaval of a magnitude unknown before in Indian history is rousing the people to a consciousness of their individual importance, loosening family, caste and village ties, changing attitudes toward authority and religious beliefs, increasing the desire for the material comforts of life and compulsively preparing the ground for new social structures demanded by an industrial society. All these variables are consciously or unconsciously playing their part in shaping the Church's pastoral policy in India. We shall, therefore, briefly trace the main trends in the complex process of economic and social advancement that are relevant to our inquiry:

    I. The Slow Pace of Industrialization
    II. The Secular State and Secularization
    III. Religious Pluralism and the Christian Minority

We shall then describe how the Church is facing the challenge and how its pastoral apostolate is being directed to secure specific objectives as a result of its awareness of these trends and their action upon its existence and development.

I

THE SLOW PACE OF INDUSTRIALIZATION

There is much talk of the rapid industrialization of India. In fact the three five-year plans were intended to set the pace by laying the foundation for self-sustaining growth in the form of increased production of steel, transport and power. The planners unfortunately never bargained for the numerous bottlenecks due to the scarcity of capital and human skill, the absence of motivation and the weight of ancient customs that have sharply retarded the expansion of the economy. It is obvious now that the transition to an industrial society will take a long time. India is still a land where the rural way of life predominates. Nearly 80 per cent of her population are concentrated in the villages. It may be that the five-year plans have concentrated so much attention on industrialization, that agricultural production has been neglected and the food grains required to feed a growing population are now in short supply. It is strange that India, an essentially agricultural country, should have to feed its population with food grains imported from the U.S.A., an industrial country.

The fact is that the agricultural methods in use in India are still primitive. The harvest depends on the monsoon rains, and if these fail, the peasants starve and workers in the city are faced with a critical shortage of essential commodities. Although irrigation schemes were taken in hand under the five-year plans, the farmers were not prepared for the change brought about by the more ample influx of water that required them to adopt new patterns of cropping. Fertilizers have not been available at the time and in the quantity needed. And the community development projects on which large amounts have been spent have failed to enthuse local initiative. The reasons for this are many. The departmental officials in charge of the scheme find it difficult to adjust themselves to the new setup that calls for great initiative and leadership by sharing the hard lot of the peasants. There are very few of the educated elite in India who would venture to live and work in the villages. They shun the rural areas, where neither schools, nor roads, nor dispensaries, nor clean drinking water can be obtained.

To brighten this somber rural picture, however, one must mention the greater contact with the outer world through radio, railway and road communications that the villages now enjoy. In every village there is a school and most of the villages are visited by the health officials. The industrial revolution has dotted the Indian landscape in many remote areas with smoking chimney stacks. The blast of sirens and the roar of machines shatter the silence of the countryside today; and the people are stirring under the impact. It is likely that on the whole the Indian masses are better fed and better clothed today than two decades ago.[1]

[1] Wilfred Malenbaum, *Prospects for Indian Development* (George

All this implies, however, that the rural parishes will remain as they are for quite some time to come. And a great amount of work remains to be done for the economic and social uplift of the rural parishioners. Many of them are tenant farmers who are weighed down by heavy debts or are day laborers who work on a pittance for others. Unemployment is an acute problem for it is only during a part of the year that they can find employment. Some of them might migrate to the large cities or towns or industrial townships in search of better prospects.

Thus, the process of transition of an agrarian community to an industrial society is going to be a long one; not only long but also slow and painful. There is no shortcut to an industrialized community especially in the new democratic societies where pockets of vested interests that arise in the course of change may become obstacles to further change. Century-old traditions cannot be transformed overnight. The law has been used in India to suppress untouchability, but the law has failed to bring about social equality. This is not to deny that the situation of the untouchables or harijans, as they are called, is not different from what it was a few years ago. Harijans today are conscious of their rights to equality and liberty under the Constitution and many of them are making efforts to raise themselves in the social scale through higher education, nonmenial employment and work in industry.

Thus, the independence of the country and its industrial development under the spur of strong nationalist feeling has released new dynamic forces in an ancient society. In former times, poverty was accepted as an exogenous factor beyond the control of economic forces to banish. Indians think differently today. The existence of a high standard of living in the West that has practically banished extreme poverty has roused expectations of achieving similar standards of well-being among the masses of the people in underdeveloped countries. And this thirst must be satisfied; they will never be content until levels of living familiar

---

Allen and Unwin, 1962), pp. 123ff.; J. P. Lewis *Quiet Crisis in India* (Asia Publishing House, 1963), pp. 155ff.

to the West become their own. From this compulsion toward a world society based on an economic equality of living standards, no pastoral preoccupations can stand apart.

II
THE SECULAR STATE AND SECULARIZATION

The second significant factor in the Indian social and political situation which vitally affects present pastoral policy is that India has been declared a secular State by her rulers after independence. Though the word "secular" is not specifically used in the Constitution, there are clauses in that historic document which prevent the State from discriminating against a citizen on the sole ground of religious belief, in respect of employment opportunities, access to certain places (usually forbidden to outcastes among the Hindus), and educational institutions. On the other hand, the State is permitted to make special provisions for the advancement of any social and educationally backward classes of citizens.

It has to be noted, however, that the concept of the secular State has arisen in Europe and America where religion has become institutionalized through the establishment of the Church. It is easy to talk and be understood in the West when reference is made to the separation of Church and State. The Church is a highly organized body with laws of its own, its own officials, obeying a central authority, even though the limitations of that authority are bound by the sphere of the temporal.

In India, Hinduism, the religion of the vast majority, can hardly be compared to a Church because it has no central organization, no hierarchy, no clear-cut demarcation between the spheres of the spiritual and the temporal. Instead caste has been the social institution, upheld and sanctioned by religious belief and tradition, that to a large extent has preserved Hinduism as we know it today. For this reason, despite the secular character of the Indian State, State legislation impinges on such religiously inspired institutions as untouchability, which has been abolished by the Constitution. Even Hindu marriage and Muslim and Christian marriage laws are being enacted by the State.[2]

Conjoined with this concept of the secular, there is at work today a new process of what we may call *secularization,* or the growth of areas of social life withdrawn from all religious influence. This is happening in India as quickly as it is taking place in the West.

The integration of society, state and religion in India under both Hindu and Muslim rule was only broken by the advent of the British. The latter carefully refrained from interference with religious observance, except in a few extreme cases such as *Sati,* where the Hindu wife immolated herself on her husband's funeral pyre. This was forbidden and the practice has disappeared. The clashes between Hindus and Muslims during British rule convinced our present leaders that only a secular State was feasible in India. The process of emancipation from religious and social control is proceeding swiftly. There is no religious instruction of any kind in State schools and, except for certain traditional ways of behavior practiced at home, children are given no moral guidance for daily living. The comparatively rapid increase in the population and the shortage of food has aroused the government to take strong measures to control the fertility rate through encouraging the people to use contraceptive methods and sterilization. Under the pressure of mass publicity, what are described as ancient sex taboos are being overthrown and a more liberal attitude toward sex is being inculcated. Though there can be no doubt that the population growth in India is an urgent problem, the publicity given to the use of contraceptives, sterilization and even abortion is likely to have a disastrous effect on sexual morality. One of the saddest consequences for our pastoral activity is going to be the near impossibility of getting people who have been brought up with such loose morals to accept the rigorous code of Christian morality in sexual matters.

But not all aspects of the growing trend toward secularization

[2] V. P. Luthera, *The Concept of the Secular State* (Oxford University Press, 1964), pp. 146ff.

are unfortunate. There is a greater readiness today to accept new knowledge and to judge of matters objectively. Old prejudices regarding liberty of action in choosing one's partner in marriage, marrying outside the caste, living in a joint family, are gradually dying out. Nationalism, the desire for equality and the banishment of poverty are some of the powerful forces at work in these rejuvenated ancient cultures. The stress is on fundamental human rights and the demand for their recognition. India is one of the few countries in Southeast Asia to have a democratic government. And if the present period of transition can be safely crossed without a political upheaval, there is every likelihood that democracy and the political implications that this method of government requires will take deep roots in the Indian soil.

III

Religious Pluralism and the Christian Minority

In India, religious pluralism is as much a basic element of the milieu in which the Church has to function as it is in Africa. And what Archbishop Blomjous of Mwanza (Tanganyika) has written about the subject applies with equal force to the situation in this country.

The 1961 Census places the total population of India at a little over 439 million. Of these, Christians number over 10.5 million, *i.e.,* about 2.44 per cent. There are over 366 million Hindus; they account for 83.51 per cent of the population. The Muslims are nearly 47 million, or about 10 per cent of the total population. Then come the Sikhs with nearly 8 million, Buddhists with over 3 million and Jains with over 2 million.

Given this overall picture, Christians can be classed as the third largest minority in India. Since the last Census of 1951, Christians have increased in number by 27 per cent. Even at this rate of growth, both by natural increase and through conversions, it might well take another forty to fifty years for the Christian population simply to double its present number, let alone to gain any percentage strength in reference to the total population.

With Archbishop Blomjous we may well ask the question: What is the theological significance of religious pluralism? What does God wish to convey to us through this multiplicity of religions? [3]

It has to be remembered further that the Christian population is split up between 6 million Roman Catholics and 4 million belonging to various Protestant denominations. This only serves to complicate the situation further. Can we expect an avalanche of conversions from either the non-Christians or the Protestants to Roman Catholicism? Is the work of the Church mainly a question of a race for numbers?

Viewing the matter from another angle, we have to realize that despite the guarantee of the Constitution, in regard to the propagation of religion, conversion to Christianity is looked upon with disfavor by the majority community, and the convert is often ostracized by members of his former community. Missionary activity is looked upon with suspicion, and although missionary zeal is highly praised and valued in modern India by non-Christians, its effects are resented when it results in attracting adherents to the religion of the missionary. Despite the growing number of indigenous missionaries, Christianity is even now regarded as a foreign religion, that somehow clashes with the cultural values of Hinduism. There are indications that these prejudices are slowly dying away, and that Christianity is being accepted as one of the religions of India. The suspicion still lingers that it taints its members, especially new Christians, with a foreign veneer. This can hardly be avoided, since Christianity is not only a religion but also a way of life, with values that are at variance with some of the deepest instincts in the Hindu mind.

On the other hand, it is no less true that, like every minority the world over, Christians in India suffer from a sense of frustration and persecution. A large majority of the community belong to the lower income groups. Many are tribals recently emancipated from their hilly surroundings and merging with the rest

[3] "Oecuménisme et Conversion," in *Informations Catholiques Internationales* (April, 1964), p. 3.

of their countrymen in a way of life that has evolved in modern
India.

In these circumstances, Archbishop Blomjous' intuitive explanation of the mission of the Church through the ages comes
as a consoling revelation. The Church is the light and the leaven
in human society. Her mission is one of bearing witness and
serving the entire human community. Not only is the Church
concerned with saving souls for heaven; she is also concerned
with humanizing the social life of man, arousing in all men the
sense of their personal responsibility, and promoting a social
order that offends the divine justice less grievously.

IV

THE ANSWER TO THE CHALLENGE

How is the Church in India facing the challenge of the social
upheavals in the society in which she lives and works? What
does she conceive her role to be in a nation where she is hope-
lessly outnumbered? What steps is she taking to prepare her
members for the task they must play in building an active and
responsible Christian community, alive to the obligations in shaping a social order more in accordance with the divine plan?

Before these questions can be answered, one point should be
made quite clear. It would be far beyond the scope of this article
to describe and evaluate the complex adjustments, however interesting and successful, on the liturgical and religio-cultural
planes that have been initiated within the Church. I think it is
much more appropriate to indicate rather the efforts made by
both hierarchy and laity to adjust their pastoral activities to the
requirements of the technological revolution overtaking the country. These form a very interesting chapter in the life of the
Church in India.

1. *The Struggle against Hunger and Disease*

In the first place, the Church is busying herself with the problem of hunger and its alleviation. In practically every diocese there has been a growing interest in seeking some solution to the gigantic task of providing the people, both Catholic and non-Catholic, with food and employment. In practically every parish throughout the land, the distribution of rice, wheat, clothes— gifts from the U.S.A., Europe and Australia—to all without concern of religious belief has become one of the regular functions of the parish. It is now being realized, however, that such distribution does not solve the fundamental problem of hunger, and malnutrition. The individual must learn to become self-sufficient and self-reliant.

This novel emphasis is especially due to the regulations governing loans and donations granted by MISEREOR—the German Bishops' Campaign against Hunger and Disease. As far as possible, projects that have for their object the increase of agricultural production either in the form of food grains, milk, vegetables, poultry, fish, etc., are given prime consideration. For these projects, MISEREOR may sometimes supply an expert from Germany to show the Indian peasant how he can increase production through the use of modern techniques of farming. With MISEREOR aid, agricultural schools have been started for the sons of the farmers. Most of these boys go back to the land. In Kerala in particular, projects for the provision of nylon nets and mechanized boats have been approved. The distribution of these articles is done through the cooperative of the fisher folk of the locality.

Land reclamation and the settling of landless laborers on reclaimed land is another type of project that is being encouraged. The formation of cooperatives of all kinds, such as marketing cooperatives, milk cooperatives, consumer cooperatives, etc., are growing in number. Catholic Charities of the United States, that formerly was mainly a distributing agency for food, has been caught up by the same idea of encouraging the recipients of its charity to undertake productive projects in order to increase the skill of the people and make them self-reliant.

The number of Catholic hospitals has been growing rapidly

in recent years. One particularly significant reason has been the establishment of the Medical Mission Sisters, founded by Mother Anna Dengel. This congregation is devoted to the care of the sick and its members are either trained nurses or doctors. Through MISEREOR aid, the Medical Mission Sisters have set up several large hospitals in India. The Catholic Hospital Association today is a powerful nucleus in India both for the training of nurses and the ethical guidance and moral influence wielded by Catholic hospitals and Catholic doctors in the medical sphere. It is one of the biggest difficulties in India to get trained medical personnel to work in the villages. Neither doctors nor nurses will volunteer for such employment. It is only the missionary sisters, both nurses and doctors, who are prepared for the sacrifice.

To make ample provision for the steady supply of such personnel is one of the objectives of the St. Luke's Medical College that has been set up in Bangalore. Dispensaries run by the nuns of various congregations are to be found in practically every large urban and rural parish. The care of the blind, the sick and the lame and the handicapped is a growing concern of the Church in India. But most of this work is confined to the pastoral zeal of the clergy and nuns.

Another important recent event that has further helped the Church in India to understand her pastoral role in a developing country has been the International Eucharistic Congress in Bombay. Preceding the Congress there was the Seminar on Food and Health. The Archbishop of Bombay, Valerian Cardinal Gracias, in his keynote speech explained the commitment of the Church to the fight against hunger and disease and to the profound motivation of the charity of Christ that urged such a pattern of service to the needy and the sick. In this crusade, Christians could unite with their brethren of other faiths and governmental agencies in a common effort. This would help to break down the barriers between men and assist them to a better understanding of each other's beliefs and motives.

The Seminar itself was not an exclusive Catholic gathering.

The Food and Agricultural Organization of the United Nations played a leading role in guiding the Seminar discussions. Their technical experts participated actively in the plenary sessions together with those from the Indian government, international and national voluntary agencies, and the Church. The participants were mainly missionaries from the rural parts of the country with experience in agricultural projects of all kinds, especially farming, the forming of agrarian cooperatives, land reclamation, irrigation, fertilizers, etc. Nutrition experts from international as well as national organizations were present, and contributed their experience toward the fight against malnutrition.

An outstanding example of pastoral foresight in the case of one region of India where social acculturation of the people has gone hand in hand with their evangelization is Chota Nagpur. In this region, the new converts to the faith belonged to the primitive tribes who lived in the hilly plateaus, compelled to seek shelter among the hills by the successive invasions from the Northwest of India. They are a fiercely independent people, though now placed among the backward classes by the Census of India. Thanks to the credit cooperative movement established by the Belgian Jesuit missionaries already as early as 1915, the grain banks or *golas,* and the legal fight for the retention of their rights to their lands, these people are rapidly taking their place in public life with a sense of being on an equal footing with other citizens of India. Chota Nagpur today accounts for over three hundred thousand Catholics, many of whom have entered the army and navy and taken up avocations in the cities and towns of Bihar.

2. *Lay Involvement*

Chota Nagpur has become an important division of the extensive industrial area that covers the states of Bihar, Orissa and West Bengal. Here coal and iron are to be found in large quantities, and the four steel mills of India that produce nearly 4 million tons of steel a year are located in this region. Many new industrial townships have sprung up in this industrial belt. The

68   ALOYSIUS FONSECA, S.J.

only comparable locality where industrialization is progressing on a similar scale is the big city of Bombay with its hinterland stretching up to Poona in the Western Ghats.

In the state of Bihar, many Catholic tribals now migrate to the industrial townships in search of employment. Similarly, Catholics from the South especially Kerala migrate to the cities of Bombay, Delhi and the industrial townships for the same purpose. A kind of diaspora on a considerable scale is taking place, and it becomes the duty of the Catholic pastor to search for his flock and minister to their needs in the new cosmopolitan centers.

Unlike in Europe, Catholic workers have not been lost to the Church in India. They still cling to their faith in the most extraordinary way and will make great sacrifices to attend to their religious duties. This is a consoling fact. The situation however, is not without its dangers. Unless the hierarchy take serious cognizance of this problem by appointing priests who have some background in the social sciences and who are sympathetic to the workers' difficulties, it might well happen that the fate of the Church in Europe will be repeated in India. Workers must be taught the social message of the Church and be trained to participate in their trade unions in a live and responsible way. Otherwise, the new social structures that are being formed might completely escape the impact and influence of the social principles of the Church.

Unfortunately, there are large industrial cities like Bombay, Calcutta, Madras and Bangalore where almost nothing has been done to tackle this problem. The Young Christian Workers Movement has been established in these cities. Somehow the Y.C.W. groups seem to lack the dynamism that was so characteristic of the J.O.C. when it was formed in Belgium over forty years ago. Perhaps the chaplains are too overburdened with routine parish duties to attend to the needs and aspirations of the young workers. On the other hand, there are a number of good Catholic labor leaders in Bombay. Quite a few of them have been trained through trade union courses organized in Bombay by the Indian Social Institute and in Jamshedpur by the Xavier Labor Relations Institute, or by contact with the publications of the Indian Social Institute. But much more needs to be done, and far more strenuously.

A decisive start to get more laymen fully involved in the sphere of pastoral activity has recently been made through the establishment of the Indian Social Institute Extension Service at Bangalore. A number of laymen are on the staff of the Institute. They are professionally equipped to manage and guide new projects financed by MISEREOR. They form a cadre of trained professional workers who are intended to be at the service of the diocese to assist in the formation of cooperatives, to guide and train local talent, and nurse approved projects during the first years of their functioning.

Obviously, in a scheme of this kind a big drawback is the necessity to provide such lay workers with the wherewithal to live and do their work without the constant anxiety of finding the means to support themselves and their families. A fund of some kind will have to be established for their maintenance. There can be no doubt, however, that their work is urgent to supply the pastoral needs of the Church, especially in developing countries like India.

One significant result of the Seminar on Food and Health mentioned above was the plan for the formation of a registered social service society in each diocese, which should employ as field workers qualified accountants with a knowledge of business management and acquainted with the work of business institutions of different sorts. Young men fresh from the universities could be trained for this purpose at the training center of the Indian Social Institute Extension Service. Higher up, the Catholic Bishops Conference of India could engage a staff of technical men qualified in agriculture, horticulture, animal husbandry, engineering, medical science, industries, home science, etc. These technicians should visit the dioceses in which self-help projects requiring the assistance of their technical knowledge might be situated. They should also visit dioceses which ask for their aid and render technical advice in drawing up and initiating schemes.

They should be assisted by the field workers of the diocese.

The role of the layman in the pastoral activity of the Church assumes a crucial position in such a program. His technical and professional competence allows him to place at the disposal of the Church a talent peculiarly his own. It is not the normal function of a cleric to prepare himself for such professional tasks. A few ecclesiastics may specialize in these particular branches of knowledge, but these fields are the special preserve of the layman and should be left to him. On the other hand, it is recognized that work of this kind requiring full-time service and missionary dedication cannot be completely voluntary. The disciple is worthy of his hire and should at least have his essential needs cared for by the Church.

3. *Ecumenism*

There is a growing awareness among the clergy, especially in the industrial belt around Chota Nagpur of this problem of transition to an industrial society and its consequences for the future of the Church.

In July 1964, there took place in Ranchi, the central town of Chota Nagpur, an orientation course for pastors in industrial areas. This course was jointly sponsored by the Ecumenical Social Industrial Institute, a Protestant venture started in Calcutta, and the Xavier Institute of Social Service, established by the Jesuits at Ranchi. Archbishop Kerketta of Ranchi and Bishop Picachy of Jamshedpur (where the great Tata Iron Steel Company is situated) represented the Catholic hierarchy. The Venerable B. Manual, Archdeacon of Calcutta, the Rev. Kenyon Wright, the Rev. Dilbar Hans represented the Protestant hierarchy. The topics for discussion were pastoral problems in industrial areas, the future of urban parishes, the role of Christians in trade unions, common action by the Churches in the social field, the Christian concept of work, problems of the family, young workers and working girls in industrial areas, etc.

Some of the basic ideas that stood out continuously were that the Christian is not called to save individuals out of this evil

world, but rather to penetrate the very structure of the new industrial society with the leaven of the Gospel. It follows that
the Church should not shy away from modern conditions and
fight a losing rear-guard battle against the world, but rather be,
in the words of the World Council of Churches, "a witness to,
and an agent of, what God is doing in this industrial society".
This task belongs to the whole People of God, primarily, however, to lay people. It is, therefore, the task of pastors to train
their lay people to be in the world without being of the world,
and to commit themselves wholeheartedly to assume leadership
—which in the Christian sense is essentially a SERVICE—in
those institutions where the future of the world is being shaped
and decided, such as the trade unions, management associations,
community-development projects, political parties, journalism
and the press.

More important than the mere exchange of ideas was the
warmth of the charity that suffused all hearts. The pastors felt
that in the modern industrial world, the call of the apostolate
and of the service of mankind, was also a call to unity among
themselves. This orientation course appears to have been an important milestone on the road to unity.

4. *The Leaven and the Light*

Nothing has been said about the extraordinary educational
work of the Church in India. Catholic schools and colleges are
well known throughout the land for the excellence of their training and the sense of discipline they maintain. This intellectual
apostolate of the Church has served to expel prejudice and has
created a moral instinct for human values in the student. It has
made the Church more acceptable in Indian society. Indeed, it
can be said that because of the schools and especially the colleges
and institutions of higher learning, the influence of the Catholic
minority is far in excess of its numbers. Of late, there have been
innovations into new fields of training. A few engineering and
technical courses have been started in the urban centers and a
couple of agricultural schools in the rural areas. Courses for

labor leaders and management executives, and the formation of Catholic associations of active Catholic trade unionists and management executives have been achieved.

There is a new bias in the training of Catholic students toward manual work and undertaking of relief activities in the slum areas of the towns and the villages. The preparation of professional social workers is undertaken in a few Catholic colleges. Research in social problems that affect developing countries in the fields of labor, the family and the urban expansion due to industrialization is the special function of the Indian Social Institute at New Delhi. But what are these efforts when compared with the millions who must somehow be made to feel the impact of the Catholic "presence".

From an analysis of the efforts at adjustment, it is clear that a large number of religious orders and congregations have played a leading part in the whole movement toward *aggiornamento*. There must be room within the Church for the free play of such initiative. The modern world is so conscious of the merits of the democratic experiment that one can hardly expect the Church not to be influenced by the obvious advantages of decentralization. In the new climate of democratic leadership, the free play for experimentation and maneuver must be allowed some opportunity for exercise. Obviously, there have to be limits, but it is wiser that the limits be placed by a group like the Committee of the Catholic Bishops of India, which consists of a large number of prelates with diverging views, rather than under a single prelate with fixed views of his own.

The remarkable initiative of the Church in the social field has roused the interest of India's Planning Commission to institute an inquiry into the motivating forces of such successful voluntary endeavor. A research officer of the Public Cooperation Department of the Planning Commission has just produced a report of an investigation into the work of the Sisters of Charity founded by Mother Teresa, who received an award from the government of India for her selfless labors on behalf of destitute men and women in the city of Calcutta.

The report has favorably impressed the officials of the Planning Commission especially by the extraordinary dedication of the Sisters of Charity to the service of the abandoned. An awareness of the mysterious spirit that inspires the heroic work of the Christian missionary and makes it far more successful than the official government projects with their vast expenditure and expert personnel is becoming evident to the men who make policy. The witness of the Church is assuming a new dimension in the developing countries through self-sacrificing service of the neighbor in helping to build a new social structure more consonant with the nature of man and human aspirations. Nor has the interest of the Planning Commission stopped with this one report. It is intended to study other outstanding efforts of Catholic charity in different parts of India and especially Bombay, the venue of the International Eucharistic Congress.

It may well be asked at this stage whether the efforts enumerated above are decisively influencing the powerful forces of change toward their proper goals? The answer, unfortunately, has to be in the negative, because these attempts of the Church are far too isolated and feeble. They merely represent the incipient stages of a realistic pastoral policy on the part of the Catholic community. They need to be strengthened and deepened and catch the imagination of Catholics themselves. The Church has an excellent social philosophy, but it needs to be so interpreted and adapted that it becomes meaningful to the leaders of India's millions and can be assimilated by them to shape and mould the social institutions through which they hope to preserve the values they now treasure most.

As M. M. Thomas writes, "There is a search for a dynamic ideology that will buttress the new pattern of social humanism. Nationalism has come into being through the struggles for national freedom. But it needs to be related to a social ideology powerful enough to fight highly entrenched vested interests. And so we have the search for a social ideology that can speak of development, social justice and personal freedom not merely as ideals, but with a sense of their relation to the ultimate nature and destiny of man and an ultimate interpretation of history. This is the situation in which the whole range of ideologies, different forms of Liberalism, Socialism, and Marxism have been battling for the soul of man; and it is this situation that shapes the thinking of man regarding the meaning of life and human salvation among the people of these many countries." [4]

Thomas also recognizes that the search for such a dynamic ideology is not peculiar to these new independent States, but is a worldwide phenomenon. Practically every country is aware of the pressures resulting from a growing sense of human solidarity toward a world community. For the creation of this new organism, a new social fabric informed by a satisfying social ethos is required. Once again the social aspects of the Christian message could become the powerful ingredient to support this new dynamic movement toward a united humanity.

CONCLUSION

In this brief essay we have endeavored to trace the main lines of the Church's pastoral policy in one of the largest developing countries, India. As has been pointed out, despite the five-year plans, with their prospect of rapid industrialization, the transition to an industrial society is going on at a comparatively slow pace. The rural parishes are still facing grave problems of acute poverty and unemployment for their members. On the other hand, new methods of farming and the use of more efficient tools, the dependence on the market, and the use of money and credit are manifestations of the technological society that is slowly making headway in the country. In the industrial areas, Catholic migrants from all parts of India are to be found. Side by side with the advance of industrialization, however, is the growing secularization of social living.

In this context, the parish will have to assume new functions

[4] *Religion and Society,* Bulletin of the Christian Institute for the Study of Religious Society (Bangalore, June, 1964), p. 11.

if it wishes to make an impact on the surrounding environment. In former times, it was sufficient to establish a school, but today this is not enough; the service of the new society must reach beyond the sphere of education and plunge into schemes that will make the farmer self-sufficient, healthy and comfortable. Nor must this be regarded as a mere seeking of material advantages for the neighbor. The conviction is growing that poverty is not an evil to be welcomed. A certain level of material prosperity is conducive to religious maturity and development.

How is the pastoral activity of the Church developing and with what consequences? Projects of a variety of types from land reclamation and the digging of wells to the formation of marketing societies in the rural areas and the provision of training facilities, agricultural and urban development through professional lay workers, are increasing in number. The international Catholic agencies that formerly provided finance for relief are now placing the emphasis on rehabilitation and development. The outcome for the Church is likely to be a laity equipped with the skills and facilities necessary for material development and an elite of lay apostles who will help to build the new social structures of an industrial society on Christian principles.

This is a fascinating program, but it has only just begun. There is still much leeway to be made. Much, too, depends on the quality of the leadership that is directing the program. There is no doubt that the extraordinary success of a part of the effort has intrigued the policy makers in the country and the motivation that can produce such heroic commitment has puzzled them. It is this opportunity and challenge that the Church in India is facing. And it is by answering the challenge in a positive manner that she can fulfill her destiny of saving society and rebuilding social institutions after the pattern intended by the creator.

Georges Cottier, O. P. / *Geneva, Switzerland*

Why Communism Appeals to Developing Countries

This article wishes to examine from the pastoral point of view what influence Communism may have on the growth of the underdeveloped countries, the primary social task for our generation. By its Marxist ideology Communism intends to provide the final and definitive solution to the problems that beset mankind. Its teaching about man, with atheism as its keynote, is in direct conflict with Christianity. Insofar as it sees the fulfillment of man on the level of history and society, it also conflicts with the social teaching of the Church. On both these grounds it is of direct interest to us.

The problem of the effective assistance given by the Communist bloc to the developing countries is a matter of economic statistics and does not concern us here. Although less than the assistance given by the industrial countries of the West, it is enough to remember that this aid is not negligible, and it has known both successes and failures. On the other hand, interpretation of a specific success or failure is difficult because it is influ-

* GEORGES COTTIER, O.P.: Born April 25, 1922 in Geneva, Switzerland, he became a Dominican and was ordained in 1951. He studied at the University of Geneva and at the Angelicum in Rome, earning his doctorate in philosophy in 1959. He is professor of philosophy at the University of Geneva, editor-in-chief of *Nova et Vetera* (Geneva), and private *peritus* to Archbishop de Provenchères of Aix-en-Provence, at Vatican Council II.

enced by far too many contingent factors. Nor should one forget that in judging some action taken by Communist States, they are often led as States to defend strictly political and economic interests that do not always logically flow from "communism". This last point becomes clearer as the rivalry between Russia and China develops. We should also take into account the influence of local Communist movements and, more generally, the kind of hearing Marxist notions receive.

If, therefore, we look on Communism as a world vision that directly inspires a way of acting, we may inquire which aspects of Communism are most likely to appeal to the elite and to the masses of underdeveloped countries. To do this, we must distinguish between ambitions and expression. We have to reject a certain number of essentially Marxist notions as basically wrong and irreconcilable with the Christian concept of life, but there can hardly be any doubt that these notions owe their success to the fact that they often give expression to genuine ambitions of our time.

First of all, Communism proclaims that today is the historic moment for the masses. Today, the *people,* too long despised and kept in subjection, are the new and authentic factor in the battle of history. Formerly treated in history as passive matter, paying with their mute sufferings for the excesses of the powerful, the people are at long last aware of their own historic task. Their interests and dignity are taken seriously, and henceforth, they are the masters of their own destiny. True, the political formulas of Communism are reduced to a rigid and totalitarian regimentation of the masses, called upon to yield to the "revolution from the top down" (since Stalin, as is known, completely reversed Marx's doctrine on this capital point). But in these pages we would rather concentrate on the hopes raised by Communist ideology than on the particular achievements of Communist powers. Now, it seems to us that by its insistence on the historic responsibility of the people, Marxist propaganda makes use of the awakening democratic sense that is one of the basic facts of modern society, and a point taken up by the most recent social encyclicals. Indeed, democracy may be defined as the recognition of the personal dignity of every individual human being, and of his positive responsibility and right to initiative in political society. But although awareness of what democracy demands is a basic fact in our contemporary society, its practical realization with all its implications is only just beginning and encounters many obstacles. In these circumstances, Communist ideology provides the frustrated masses with a way of expressing themselves and with a means of exercising pressure.

Secondly, the appeal of Communism or Marxism blends well with the appeal of what we shall call rationalism or, more simply, reason, by which we mean man's new awareness of the ample power of his own intelligence when applied to the systematic exploration of the world and of himself, as both an individual and a social being. Such knowledge is not meant to be for its own sake: knowledge is power. It aims at what is practical, and, therefore, at the transformation of the material world in the service of man. By his reason man can control himself and his environment: he is the master. His reason is also a means of conquest: to know is to dominate, and the man who has a scientific knowledge of nature and society can control his destiny.

He enters into full possession of his human dignity because instead of passively undergoing the process of history as in the past, he controls it. But the control of history implies that man is capable of creating his own happiness, which will be genuine precisely insofar as it is not a gift from somebody else, but forged by himself. In this way rationalism acquires an ethical dimension that is an essential part of it. "Scientific socialism" appeals because it makes reason appear as sovereign, the master of destiny and the creator of happiness. It must be added that the accent falls on society as the principal object of rational activity. This society is man himself, since in the Marxist view man is essentially a social being.

It is vital to observe that in this view the universality of reason acquires an eschatological dimension: the society that is being built coincides with the kingdom of reason. But in order to bring about this historic enterprise, Communism does not appeal to the present state of "reason" in every individual, which provides that all men may become "reasonable". It does not start from the premise that common sense is the most common thing in the world. Reason, here, is a militant reason that has to overcome the opposition of the forces of darkness. In this battle there is a party of reason that is precisely the party of the masses. In this way, the assertion of the sovereignty of reason has the advantage of mobilizing forces for the battle. Consequently, violence by no means represents the irruption of irrationality and chaos into the field of history, but rather the advance of reason, as long as this violence serves the party of reason.

Paradoxically, the mythical notion of the proletariat is the key to this total rationalism. Violence is justified while reason's progress feeds on passion and aggressivenes. Reason's progress finds no guarantee in the peaceful diffusion of "light" that would compel conviction by its very clarity; it is snatched from a battle-field where reason is opposed by the forces of "reaction" that try to bar its way. More, even, than a battle *for* reason, it is in itself a battle waged *by* reason.

The link, then, between Party action and the rational approach is forged by the conviction that Party action follows the direction of history. This conviction stimulates the attempt to provide an "objective", "scientific" analysis of the contemporary historical situation. In the first phase reason tries to establish a critical diagnosis of the forces engaged in the present contingency. Here we can find an indication that the appeal of Marxism lies more in what it claims to achieve and its planned approach than in its possible results. This explains why it continues to appeal in spite of relevant and scientifically decisive criticisms of Marx's thought: Marx analyzed the industrial society of the West in the 19th century. The period that stretches from him to Stalin and Mao has seen substantial changes in this doctrine. Certain key notions, such as class or infrastructure, are too vague to allow of a strict and realistic investigation. Concrete facts have belied a certain number of "laws" and forecasts, etc.

In spite of this, many still take the Marxist interpretation as valid. Perhaps they do so because it provides a kind of framework that helps them to make some plausible sense out of social and historical matters, at least if they limit themselves to a broad and rough outline. Thus, the suggested categories give a certain logical coherence to the object analyzed. The more so, since behind propositions that are debatable when taken literally, there lies sometimes an intuition that is correct. For example, the theory about infrastructure and superstructures is neither acceptable nor applicable in its preconceived rigidity; yet there is something worthwhile in the hypothesis that society is all-embracing and implies a process of interaction that binds all its components together.

Again, when Marxists apply the law of dialectics to social conditions, it becomes clear that the class struggle is a priority and that the framework of society is based on a master-slave relationship. This is the relationship that the deprived masses do, in fact, experience, politically, socially and psychologically in most of their daily life. When people talk about international relations or national politics they show that there is no more social harmony on those fronts than in the factory or in the local neighborhood. Everywhere the strong crush the weak, and disillusioned people add: "In their place we would do the same". And so Marxist criticism looks convincing: at first sight, some of its concepts seem to correspond to elementary experience. Thanks to that framework, man has the impression that he can explain himself to himself, that he can take stock of his true situation and of his own power to change the world.

This appeal to critical reason is but a first phase. The second is concerned with constructive reason, and is more important. Since history is a rational process, "scientific socialism" is man's means of guiding it. The romantic enthusiasm for the Revolution or the assertion of the quasi-messianic mission of the proletariat, were powerful factors in the rise of the movement from its beginnings until the end of the last war. However, these aspects of Marxism are discarded today. But it is probably true to say that the principal appeal of Communism to the underdeveloped world may be described with one word: the Plan, if we mean by that, the total planning of society.

Both a myth and a concept, the Plan represents precisely that emergence of reason brought about through the organized and "conscious" collective effort of the proletariat and the peasantry: it is opposed to an irrational society where man exploits man. This idea of a total plan presupposes two other notions: the rationalization of society, and the idea that this rationalization must of necessity be total. These notions appeal particularly to the political elite because the problem of development is seen as an all-embracing one that can only be solved by a strong, centralized government, capable of carrying the masses with it. To frame this Plan in a one-party system, then, appears to be the best way of achieving its development, particularly during the delicate initial phase.

To men worried about getting things done and rightly impatient because of the urgency of the tasks, freedom appears a luxury that only rich countries can afford. It is something they will talk about later when the people are fed and clothed, have become literate and are fully employed. Moreover, these men are wary—and not always without reason—of introducing a parliamentary system to the exclusive advantage of a privileged class. "Freedom" too often means leaving complete license to the strong. This, again, the poor know by experience: they have always been victims of a hoax. From this point of view, the theme of the hypocrisy of "official democracy" is still very relevant.

Finally, and this ethical and psychological aspect is decisive, the Plan embodies the advancement of human dignity and pride: the people themselves achieve their own emancipation by their own energy and their own sacrifices.

Nevertheless, the appeal of Marxism is more than that of a formula or political recipe to allow a society to make effective progress on the way to development. If this "technocratic" aspect is a determining factor, it is not the only one. For, in the Marxist and Communist perspective, the Plan chosen by any given country is not one possibility among others. It is part of a universal movement and is integrated in the solidarity of the international proletariat. In other words, Communism brings to a certain technique of power and economic rationalization the dimension of history. Marxist political activity goes beyond its own particular contribution and is part of the movement that leads the whole of mankind to its total emancipation; it takes part in the building up of man. Its concrete political activity is absorbed, as part of the historical evolution of the world, by the irreversible current that leads history to its final fulfillment, its *eschaton*.

Marxism has been called, not without reason, a "secular religion". Thus, the forces of emotion are pressed into the service of concrete tasks, often trite and unrewarding, that can be undertaken in a spirit of enthusiasm, at least for a period. It is probable that some political leaders find this aspect of Communism attractive, not because they themselves are convinced Marxists, but because they recognize the need for such a "social force" as provided by an ideology. Without it, indeed, how can one make the masses play their part enthusiastically in the realization of the Plan?

In this perspective the historical dimension becomes a psychological stimulant to spur on the masses. One may observe that the various types of fascism have also used ideology as a source of social dynamics. But fascist ideology is a limited ideology, based on nationalism and exalting irrational forces, while Communism aims at something universal and rests on a rationalistic assumption. In fact, however, these contrasts are not clear-cut, and Soviet ideology under Stalin, for instance, had swallowed a strong dose of nationalism. The various forms of neo-Marxism that have sprung up here and there among the young nations thrive, more often than not, on a symbiotic existence with nationalism. Behind the differences one discovers the common need of a myth, in the sense given to it by Georges Sorel, in order to provide psychological motive power for action by the masses.

Although the vision of Marxism looks mainly toward the construction of the future, it also covers the past. Precisely because historical significance is attributed to the Communist Plan, it must be situated in the process of history. From beginning to end it must follow the dialectical rhythm and proceed by those qualitative leaps forward that are the revolutions. The building of the new society is, therefore, in antithesis to what was denied by the old one. So the movement of history is marked by breaks, increasingly violent, as the class struggle proceeds, until there remain only the two final antagonists: the capitalist bourgeoisie and the proletariat.

This historical scheme hides another one, psychological in nature, in the sense that it betrays a Manichaean view of the historical process: the future, bearing the promise of an integral humanism, conflicts with a past that stands irrevocably condemned. Whatever the Marxist affirms is accompanied by a criticism of the past and its legacy. As such, it takes on the aspect of salvation. The past represents alienation, the ruin of man, while Communist action aims at "reappropriation", recovery, at the return (*Zurückführung*) of man *who was lost*. A ruthless trial of the past and of the status quo strengthens the will to fight. Christianity and "Christian civilization" (no distinction is made between these two) provide a preeminent target. Christianity has not only failed, but has led mankind astray with illusory solutions: this is one of the meanings implied in "alienation".

The terms "progressive" and "conservative" serve to express this opposition. They designate two conceptions of historical reality and, consequently, two attitudes toward life. The conservative conception is one of "fixity": the "will of God" or the laws of destiny are responsible for all that happens inevitably. The human attitude that derives from this view will be one of passivity, of submission, of resignation, of accepting whatever happens.

In contrast, the progressive, armed with "scientific" knowledge, knows that evolution is the law of the world. An inner dynamism carries reality toward progress. Man looks toward the future, which he helps to build by his own conscious action. He no longer accepts as inevitable what he knows to be in his power to change. There is something of a caricature in this systematic opposition, first formulated by Engels. But we should not underrate the power of its appeal. When applied to societies that are not yet industrialized, it suggests certain norms for a plausible diagnosis. These societies seem almost paralyzed by the brutal impact of problems created by their contact with an industrially and technically minded civilization. Their values and patterns of behavior are transmitted by custom, and determined by an older generation that has the solemn duty of passing on the legacy of previous generations. Through this repetition of what has been done from time immemorial, the young are fitted into a system of perfect continuity.

The contact with industrialized societies is disturbing because of the new problems it creates and because of the new mentality that it spreads, namely, the new sense of the critical and inventive power of reason. This causes a radical break between the generations. The inheritors are no longer interested in inheriting what appears senseless to them; worse than that, they mercilessly criticize their elders, who cannot understand their sudden uselessness: are the taboos of the past not responsible for the wastage of centuries? So a conflict arises between the violent resentment of the younger ones and the awkward, irrelevant, automatic self-defense of the older conservative elements.

By its very nature, a society based on custom, does not reflect upon itself; it transmits its values automatically, and not by deliberation. If such a society does not collapse of its own accord, its self-defense is bound to be total, *i.e.,* blind and incapable of distinguishing what is genuine in this inheritance from what is the result of apathy, corruption or routine. Moreover, what it defends is no longer quite the same as what it believes in, because unwittingly it has already undergone the influence of contact with the outside. It is a traumatic society, clinging to a vanishing past. On the other hand, the rising generation is sorely tempted to liquidate the past en bloc in the name of the "revolution". This tendency explains the controversy with religion as "opium of the people". In Marxist logic this notion is inspired by atheism, and the connection between the two is vital. But this connection is less obvious to many militants and sympathizers.

Within the limits of Catholic underdeveloped countries, we can see that this atheistic view concentrates on a certain sociological image of Catholicism insofar as it is inextricably bound up with a social situation doomed to disappear: the feudal mentality, the ties with the wealthy landowners, the conservative attitude, the absence of any effort to deal with the prevailing ignorance and misery, the lack of human culture among the clergy, the parasitic character of a number of inactive religious communities whose rule of poverty has become an anachronism, etc. And so the Church itself appears as part of the forces of reaction. It is obvious that one of the most imperative needs for the *aggiornamento* lies in this domain. What kind of sociological image does the Church present in this or that country? Does it reflect the true ecclesial tradition in the sense of evangelical charity, constantly aware of the needs of the poor? Or does it reflect the routine and the all too human abuses that contradict its true nature? For the *aggiornamento* is born of a supernatural alertness that can cope with the constant readjustment required by the demands of the Gospel and current social changes.

There is yet another element that fans the flame of revolution. It is closely linked with the preceding one and its causes lie perhaps still deeper. It might be described as the despair of noble and generous sentiments. Behind this despair lies a profound pessimism that affects the mainsprings of human activity within the framework of society as it actually exists. Before man is master of this society, he is conditioned by it; to it he owes his goodness or his malice, so that the pessimism concerning human persons is matched by an almost boundless trust in institutions.

It is said that, as a religion preaching charity, Christianity has failed: after two thousand years, man has not become any better. A morality based on charity is perhaps a noble dream, but it has no grip on reality; it is incapable of solving the real problems, and finally, like all dreams, it is harmful because it diverts man's attention from his real tasks. We turn to this dream of brotherhood and gentleness with a certain nostalgia. Above all, we do not trust it: too often "kindness" has been used hypocritically to cover up evil by complacency and complicity. In short, Christianity has not been true to its word: it is the great swindle and the great deception.

Effective action must begin by facing reality, and, we should have the courage to admit it, the law of reality is the law of violence. The widespread conviction that only violence is effective is, I suggest, the result of historic justice. Political amorality, indeed, is not the prerogative of Marxism; it is upheld by a long tradition in Western thought. The concrete awareness that Christian morality also extends to political practice has hardly begun to penetrate the Christian mentality seriously. For centuries Christian society has, for all practical purposes, accepted a *de facto* divorce between a Christian morality restricted to private life and a behavior of society based on violence and trickery.

Faced with this situation, some may well think that the avowedly brutal methods of violence showed courage and an intellectual integrity that dispenses with hypocrisy and calls a spade a spade. In fact, Christian thought ought to turn itself to the urgent task of discovering adequate methods that secular society can use in its actions.

This notion of the effectiveness of violence also seems to appeal to men rendered impatient by the urgency of things to be done in the social field. The immemorial, dumb patience of the poor has been nothing but a protracted deception; now that man knows the extent of his power, he will tolerate no further delays in his rebellion. Should we not see in this, too, historic justice? How easily we have resigned ourselves to the misery of others, through apathy, shortsightedness, lack of zeal, or unconcern.

In this same context, Christians are accused of indulging in half-measures, ineffectual declarations of goodwill and futile scruples. Their intention to help the poor falls short because they also intend to spare vested interests and to win the support of the powerful. The question of property proves it. It is true, according to the Church's teaching, that property is, so to speak, the economic field in which a human person can live and exercise his responsibility. But what has been done about the exploitation and contortion of this teaching when it has been used to bolster up the power of those already in possession? Compared with what looks like a dishonest compromise, Communism offers itself as the movement that is not afraid of radical solutions and is the first to attack the real wrongs of society. The very severity of this radicalism has, of course, found widespread response.

At the moment, the Communist movement passes through a serious crisis. In the light of the development of industrial societies its most lucid thinkers begin to wonder how well-founded some of its classical theses are. Thermonuclear war looms on the horizon, creating for the leaders problems that Marxism had not foreseen. Lastly, the conflict between the U.S.S.R. and China may well upset the universalist ambitions of the movement. An evolution, therefore, is certainly possible, but we would be wrong to rely on it passively.

Where Communism is in power it generally deceives the masses. Here we have only considered its appeal to developing countries. No doubt, it has been able to channel the profound yearnings of these peoples, and consequently realize the best elements of its vitality during the phase of its conquest. This conquest is a challenge thrown out to Christians. They have to take more seriously those demands that need the light of faith and the chastening of grace to give them a genuine answer and to save them from disastrous deviations.

But this challenge can only be taken up effectively if the masses recover their lost confidence in the Church. The Church is the home of the humble and the poor. How is it that millions of baptized human beings cannot recognize it today? Is it not because some sociological aspects are so far from being signs of the mystery of the Church that they have created a tragic misunderstanding? Institutions, behavior, a style of living also speak a language. But the Church's language is by nature apostolic and not esoteric. Appearances, therefore, must speak in all simplicity to the people, to whom the Gospel is directed through the Church.

PART II

BIBLIOGRAPHICAL
SURVEY

François Houtart/*Brussels, Belgium*

Jean Remy/*Brussels, Belgium*

A Survey of Sociology as Applied to Pastoral Work

I

SOCIOLOGY AND PASTORAL WORK

Like psychology, sociology is based on the study of man in his concrete reality.[1] But while psychology tries to understand the human person through the various elements that influence him, sociology is directly concerned with the overall aspects of his life in society. Its function is, therefore, to explain the origin, development and disturbances of collective phenomena. Among other things it is concerned with the development of groups, their aims, the ways in which they act and their organization, taking into account the total environment that encircles and provides them with certain opportunities for action while excluding others.

L. Dingemans has defined (qualifying this as a provisional definition) pastoral work as "the activity of the Church whereby moved by the Holy Spirit she visibly fulfills the mission that

[1] Material for this article has been provided by R. Duocastella, of the Institute of Pastoral Sociology of Barcelona; W. Goddijn, of the Dutch Pastoral Institute; N. Greinacher, formerly Director of the Center for Pastoral-Sociological Research, Essen; N. Lacoste, of the University of Montreal; R. Scarpati, of the Socio-Religious Documentation Service, Rome; A. Spencer, of the Center for Socio-Religious Research, London; B. Tonna, of the Center for Socio-Religious Research, Malta; C. Traulé, of the Center for Socio-Religious Studies, Lille, and the bibliography published by E. Pin and H. Carrier, of the International Center for Social Research of the Gregorian University, Rome, entitled, *Sociologie du Christianisme—Bibliographie internationale* (Sociology of Christianity —an International Bibliography) and published by the Gregorian University Press (Rome, 1964).

Christ has entrusted to her and pursues the realization of the Father's saving purpose for creation".[2]

Here pastoral activity is taken in the broad sense: it embraces all activity through which the Church fulfills her proper mission. It excludes, therefore, all objectives either not connected with this mission or only connected by sheer accident. It is, then, a matter of finding out which forms of activity are most suitable for the Christ-given mission of the Church: "Go therefore and make disciples of all nations . . . Teach . . . Baptize . . . You shall be my witnesses . . ."

Although this specific mission belongs to every Christian who, as a member of Christ's Church, is given both grace and responsibility for that purpose, it is, nevertheless, the special responsibility of the hierarchy. The contribution, therefore, made by sociology to pastoral activity, is in no way a substitute for those whose specific task it is to make decisions and to give directives. But like every practical science, it can provide elements that will help to make an intelligent choice because of better knowledge. In this sense a pastoral activity that tries to extend the criteria it needs, must, therefore, look not only to sociology but also to other sciences which may throw additional light on its problems, such as psychology, social psychology, human economics, human geography, etc.

Next, we must specify what kind of contribution sociology can make to pastoral activity. The problem is well illustrated by an anecdote told by the Jesuit, E. Pin: "Some years ago, at a small meeting of sociologists and priests, a parish priest asked: 'My question is no doubt somewhat naïve, but of what use is this inquiry?' There were two diametrically opposed replies. One sociologist bluntly replied: 'None whatever.' Another, equally sure of himself, said: 'But, Monsieur le Curé, every kind of use.' There was laughter and some kind of explanation, but it is no exaggeration: there were obviously two different points of view." [3]

[2] L. Dingemans, "La Pastorale et ses buts généraux," in *Evangéliser* 17 (1962), p. 247.
[3] E. Pin, "Sociologie ou Pastorale?" in *Revue de l'Action Populaire* (1959), p. 589.

This anecdote suggests a double distinction: the contributions themselves may be short-term or long-term contributions, and apart from these contributions there is the need to transfer the sociological diagnosis to pastoral therapeutics.

A given sociological investigation may help to verify a hypothesis that would assist the systematic analysis of de-christianizing factors in the modern world. In such a case the investigation would introduce a concrete new element into the long-term process of scientific systematization, but its short-term contribution to pastoral activity would be of relatively little importance. Only later on will such a scientific beginning formulate pastoral questions that may well be much more basic than the pastoral problems with which priests begin today.

On the other hand, some inquiries that would hardly affect scientific systematization might well be of great and immediate importance for such priests insofar as they reveal the complexity of the social situations in which they find themselves. Such sociological observations are only possible by again using the cumulative result of previous scientific work. In this case, sociological analysis merely shows how a particular local situation reflects a condition of which sociologists already know the component factors and the way these operate. Other sciences, too, show that immediate application is made possible only by basic scientific treatment. To a man of action one can only offer a simple and clear diagnosis when it is solidly founded on scientific results.

Priests and lay people without special sociological formation should beware of [4] trying to solve problems concerning their parish or association by simply using some good inquiry guide. The information they collect may satisfy a certain curiosity but is not always helpful for further action. This is particularly so where the sociological phenomena demand something more than a superficial treatment.

The two different methods of approach, mentioned above, often run side by side in one study. It often happens, for instance,

[4] Similar observation in Pin, *op. cit.*, p. 595.

in urban or regional studies. On the one hand, results of previous studies are used again while, on the other, such a special study helps to advance general knowledge on some particular point.

There is, therefore, an intimate and complex relationship between fundamental sociology and its application. This becomes even clearer when we analyze the connection between a sociological diagnosis and the pastoral cure.

When a priest calls in a sociologist for his own orientation, his questions are not normally the subject matter of sociological observation. Some transposition is required. Let us take the case of an industrial area inhabited by people of various nationalities. The clergy want the sociologist to tell them whether to pursue their pastoral work on the basis of integration or individual nationalities. The sociologist cannot make this the subject of his observation. This is the fault of so many inquiries conducted by Catholic Action movements. These often draft a questionnaire on the basis of apostolic problems and put down questions such as: "What do you think of common masses for people of different nationalities?" The sociologist will start from a very different point. He will begin by collecting the facts he needs to answer the question put by the clergy. He will first try to see the problem as a whole with the help of some interviews, and then will perhaps start an inquiry on whether these people want to leave the district as soon as possible or whether they want to settle down there. He will then try to define the causes and consequences of the factual situation. In this way he will discover decisive elements for the solution of the pastoral problem. But this requires a new transposition. The result of the sociological diagnosis must be translated into terms of pastoral work, and this may well change the light in which the clergy first saw their problem.

This last point may be illustrated by another example. Some parish priests in a town might ask the sociologist: "Theologically a parish should be a community. How do we set about creating a 'community'?" [5] For his answer the sociologist will begin by

[5] The word "community" appears in quotation marks because it would require too much to explain within the scope of this article.

looking for the elements required for the development of a group: occasions for contact and new relationships, etc. But as he proceeds more and more obstacles accumulate. So he finds himself forced to ask the parish priest or the theologian: "Are you quite sure that this is a theological need? This concept, which you put forward as a theological one, admirably suits the social structure of a rural environment, so much so that one may well ask whether this theological concept was not inspired by typical rural traditions. But it is frankly opposed to the modern urban evolution." With this question sociological analysis contributes to the renewal of the whole pastoral problem. The short-term and long-term contributions of sociology to pastoral activity can only be the fruit of a constant dialogue. The pastoral problem thus helps to make basic research more fruitful, but this research must in turn contribute to pastoral renewal.

This sociological contribution, however, is not limited to the organization of sociological research. This is a primary factor but not necessarily the most important from the pastoral point of view, particularly where short-term results are required. The sociologist can intervene as adviser with all the knowledge at his disposal. Thus he can be of use at conferences, helping to reframe certain questions or marking off certain developments by pointing out sociological support and sociological obstacles. This contribution is of course not easily appreciated by those who are naïve. We shall come back to this later on.

Sociology can also play an important part in the training of the clergy, either in seminaries or in pastoral organizations and conferences. First of all, it teaches the priests to observe before they make a moral judgment. Are they not too often inclined, when faced with an unexpected new situation, to judge in a way that makes scientific observation useless? For instance, has it not been said too glibly that the decline in the birthrate is due to a lack of generosity? In that case, there is nothing else to do but to exhort the flock to show more moral sense. Observation, however, of the changes affecting parents might have shown that formerly children were a source of income at an early age while today they remain a liability until a much later age. Thus it is very possible that parents have become more generous although they have fewer children. The first judgment, therefore, shows a lack of charity toward the parents and the consequent appeal to generosity is pastorally unsatisfactory. This may cause discouragement among the clergy.

Sociological orientation will also create a habit of mind and help the priest to formulate a number of questions that will enable him to react more positively when confronted with day-to-day sociological phenomena.

Finally, the habit of reading the conclusions of social religious research will prove immediately useful when pastoral decisions are to be taken.

II

THE SCOPE OF SOCIOLOGICAL RESEARCH IN RELIGION
AND PARTICULARLY IN CATHOLICISM

On the basis of work done in many countries, I shall first indicate the basic approaches, after which we shall concentrate on a group of special problems more directly concerned with pastoral activity.

1. *Basic Approaches*

An important part of religious sociology was started without any relation to pastoral problems. This was often done by authors who studied the influence of religion on the general equilibrium of society. They were, therefore, concerned with what the American sociologist R. K. Merton[6] called "the hidden functions" of religion, *i.e.,* the effects of the religious phenomenon on social life, although these effects are neither intended nor viewed as such by the religious authorities concerned. Religion can create group solidarity, an aspect often underlined by ethnologists. It can also enhance social status, and as such religion becomes a factor in social evolution. In this connection one is reminded of Marx's analysis and of Weber's famous thesis on Protestantism and the rise of capitalism.

---

[6] R. K. Merton, *Social Theory and Social Structure* (Glencoe, Ill., 1957).

Working along the same lines but limiting the scope of their investigations, others have studied the influence that membership in a religious group has on various types of behavior within one society. Does such membership affect, for instance, the size of a family, business morality, etc.? This was the approach taken by Lenski in his *The Religious Factor*.[7]

On the other hand, fundamental religious sociology, based on pastoral needs, has developed in a very different way. It shows how concrete activity can help in building up a science. Hard facts, such as de-christianization or religious indifference, create pastoral problems from which students could start to examine the influence of the general social environment on the behavior, mentality, or membership of a religious group. A thorough investigation into attendance at Sunday worship can pin down certain factors such as why in some districts of Belgium laborers have ten times less chance (in terms of the theory of probability) of practicing their religion than university graduates. Similar facts have led to a number of hypotheses on the conflict between a religion characterized by a pre-technological society and the values and standards created by a technological society. Thus a more sensitive awareness of the contemporary world leads one to question a presentation of the religious message and pastoral habits rooted in a different culture. But this makes it also possible to specify systematically what the contemporary world expects of religion.

This same starting point leads to religious phenomenology, that is, the specific meaning of religion that prevents it from being reduced to just another kind of social institution. This was the line of research undertaken by such authors as J. Wach and C. Mensching.[8] This type of work requires, perhaps more than any other, the cooperation of sociologists, philosophers and the-

---

[7] G. Lenski, *The Religious Factor* (New York, Doubleday, 1961).

[8] J. Wach, *Sociology of Religion* (Chicago, 1944, and London, 1947), French tr. *Sociologie de la religion* (Paris, Payot, 1955), German tr. *Religionssoziologie* (Tübingen, Motir, 1951), Mexican tr. *Sociologia de la Religión* (Mexico D.F., Fondo de Cultura Economica, 1958); C. Mensching, *Soziologie der Religion* (Bonn, Röhrenscheid, 1947), French tr. *Sociologie religieuse* (Paris, Payot, 1951).

ologians. This may be of strategic importance for the future of religion because it makes it possible to extricate religion from the transitory context in which it may appear in a given situation.

After the study of the mutual influence that religion and society exert upon each other, a new set of questions arises. Because religion pursues its own ends, it is bound to constitute a definite, organized group that, in turn, demands a number of specific functions. These functions, however, develop in a social context. For instance, in a modern urban area the priest's prestige is on the decline, while that of other social functions is on the increase. This leads one to examine what functions Christians primarily attribute to the priest. Starting with such questions one can gradually build up a sociology of religion as an organized group with its own social structure, its own allocation of functions and its own way of functioning.

2. Sociological Questions More Directly Connected with Pastoral Problems

These basic approaches allow us with more care to pose problems that are more directly pastoral. Moreover, the observation of these problems will help religious sociology with a better elaboration of its basic data, according to the discussion outlined above.

In this pastoral context, sociology can proceed on two lines, which may cover each other. It is rather a matter of two different points of view that give rise to a different classification of the same studies. One approach ranges these studies in view of their possible application; the second groups them according to their main objects.

The studies may bring about *a better awareness of changes and concrete situations*. This is the aim of most inquiries into the matter of religious practice. Before these inquiries, urban clergy were aware of the existence of de-christianization, but crowded churches on Sundays created a certain illusion. This illusion was the more easily accepted since one could not estimate the number of those who were absent. Investigation revealed, however, that in most European towns Catholics are in the minority. Other inquiries showed the importance of the fact that many attend Sunday services outside their parish. Statistics also pointed to other problems, such as the distribution of the clergy in urban or rural areas according to their religious functions; the analysis of the problem of priestly vocations, or their distribution as has been done in Latin America. In The Netherlands, the Catholic Social Ecclesiastical Institute (KSKI), which has produced a fair number of statistical studies, has dealt with mixed marriages and the distribution of religious groups, among other things.

Even at this stage, sociological observation does not limit itself to numerical data. For instance, in certain countries female religious are appreciated for their individual devotion to their work. But at the same time there is, even among the clergy, little esteem for the female religious in general. The discovery that individual devotion cannot neutralize an overall negative impression, cannot be made only with simple statistics.

Other studies did not start by marking off a typical sociological fact, but with situations that are already known, the *causes and development* of which must still be analyzed. This often demands a study in depth. These are also very important for a pastoral concern that is not content with stating the fact of de-christianization, for example, but wants to find out what to do about it. Here we may mention the work of E. Golomb, Director of the Pastoral-Soziologisches Institut of Essen, on the Ruhr; of the Jesuit, E. Pin, on social classes and religious practice; of the Center for Socio-Religious Research in Brussels, on the urban area of Charleroi; of J. Laloux on the region of Seraing, and of E. Pin on Latin America. These are but a few examples. These studies mainly concentrate on explaining a phenomenon that has been duly observed.

Other works are directed to the *reorganization of pastoral work*. Starting from the changes that have taken place in a given region and in the situation of the Church there, they suggest possible solutions, in line with the demands of both theologians and pastoral workers. An example of this kind of study may be found in the conclusion of the work on Charleroi.[9] Most of F. Boulard's studies also come under this heading. Finally, many studies on parochial planning also belong to this group. The most interesting are those published by the Dutch KSKI, the Belgian Research Center, and the Austrian Institute.[10]

Another classification can be made according to the object of the study. All these objects may, of course, correspond to one of the three approaches indicated above, but in the Bibliographical Supplement (Section A, pp. 104-110, at the end of this article) this is not taken into consideration.

<h3 style="text-align:center">III</h3>

THE IMPLICATIONS FOR PASTORAL WORK

As has been said, religious sociology is not merely a matter of statistics, although these are indispensable in discovering certain facts and developments. Without them, these facts would either pass unnoticed or be contorted because they are not clearly understood as a whole. Thus, an inquiry into Sunday attendance in the urban area of Charleroi revealed that 45 percent of practicing Catholics went to mass in seven central churches, although there were about fifty places of worship in the area, a fact the clergy were not aware of.

Nor would it be right to think that this type of sociology consists in reshuffling the groupings of these statistical facts. More subtle studies are necessary to define the behavior, attitudes and feelings that spring from life in a group, from belonging to certain communities or from certain social situations. Such studies help fundamentally to shape a certain *concept of man*. In the end they will eliminate that certain naïveté which makes people think that these matters simply depend on individual decisions, regardless of any other factors. This idea is often inspired by a

[9] L. Dingemans and F. Houtart, *Pastorale d'une région industrielle* (Brussels, Les Editions du Cep, 1964).

[10] *Pfarr-und Kirchenplanning für Wiener Neustadt. Forschung und Planningstelle* (Vienna, Internationales Katholisches Institut für Kirchliche Sozialforschung, 1951).

pastoral attitude. A priest often thinks that an appeal to generosity is enough to put people back on the path of righteous-
ness. How many priests think that the values dominating social
life find their origin in some teaching? They are painfully aston-
ished when it is explained to them that new values are due to
very different and much more general processes.

Detailed statistics already indicate problems of this nature.
Properly compiled statistics make it possible to foresee, within
a narrow percentage margin, how many suicides will take place
next year in a given country. But, although one can estimate
the overall importance of this phenomenon, one cannot say to
which individuals this will apply. How can one understand this
unless one has included in the explanation the influence of individual situations?

Another example, already mentioned, is that of the declining
birthrate which ought not to be blamed on individual moral
shortcomings. Is this not the fault of a pastoral approach that
seeks to remedy a situation by appealing to the responsibility
and isolated efforts of individuals? One should, of course, not
deny the part played by individual responsibility, but a simplistic
attitude toward the mechanism of social life is too serious a fault
in a world like ours where wide social changes proliferate. These
changes originate mainly in the changing environment that conditions the individual. No doubt, such collective facts are subject to moral judgment, and this is one of the basic tasks of the
Church. But the Church cannot make such a judgment through
its ministers unless it first knows the facts of social reality. Moreover, in the case of a negative judgment that demands a reaction,
one should not indulge in inadequate remedies.

This perspective, which may appear new to some, has pro-
voked opposition in the name of human liberty and the spontaneous action of the Holy Spirit. Is this not an unwarranted in-
trusion into the domain of the sacred? Other reasons have been
brought up to reinforce the opposition. By helping to understand
how the changes come about, sociology has become an instrument of transformation, and this has frightened some people.

Theologians have been heard to declare that contact between theology and the human sciences might provoke transformations of the same kind as those caused by introducing history into theology. Such arguments, as well as the inadequacy of sociological contributions at the start, have created obstacles. Sociology will only gradually receive the acknowledgment that is its due.

IV

ORGANIZATION OF RESEARCH CENTERS

Systematic research is not possible without organization.[11] This is done more and more in research centers and by teams. A study of religious sociology would show that the first countries to go ahead with it were those that already possessed a tradition in matters of Catholic organization (The Netherlands since 1946, Austria, Germany, Belgium, Great Britain), and that the response to sociological research among religious authorities went hand in hand with concern for pastoral renewal: France, the Walloon provinces of Belgium, The Netherlands, Chile, French Canada, the Congo, certain parts of Italy, Spain, Portugal and today in most other countries.

There are two Catholic international organizations:

1. The *International Conference of Religious Sociology*, founded in Louvain in 1946 by Canon Leclercq. Its headquarters are in Brussels, and it brings together students of religious sociology. Although open to men of action who are interested, it is meant mainly to assist research workers by arranging regular meetings and conferences on a theme of sociological theory. Every third year it organizes a congress. The last two congresses took place in Bologna (1959) on the theme, "Religion and Social Integration", and in Königstein (Germany, 1962) on "Psychological and Sociological Aspects of Church Membership".

2. The *International Federation of Social and Socio-Religious Research Institutes* (FERES), founded in Brussels in 1958 by

[11] F. Houtart, *Sociologie et pastorale* (Paris, Fleurus, 1963).

those countries that had organized centers at the time. Its headquarters, too, are in Brussels. It groups organizations, not individual persons, and has affiliated centers in The Netherlands, Germany, Great Britain, Belgium, France, Malta, Canada, Mexico, Colombia, Chile, Brazil, Argentina, Japan, Tanganyika, Congo, Norway. The centers for religious statistics in Germany and Spain are associate members and several new centers have applied for affiliation; these are Panama, Bolivia, India and the Philippines. A few non-Catholic centers have applied for affiliation as corresponding members. In view of the increased activity in Latin America, a special section has been set up for that continent at Bogotá.

Activity has also spread to the publishing field. Many Catholic periodicals now accept socio-religious studies. In some countries sociologists circulate periodically duplicated notes among themselves, particularly in Italy, France, Belgium and Norway.

Finally, both international institutions have their own publication. The International Conference of Religious Sociology publishes a *Bulletin de Liaison* for its members and provides information about developments in this field; the International Federation of Social and Socio-Religious Research Institutes publishes *Social Compass,* an international review of socio-religious studies. It also produces a bulletin for its own use. *Social Compass,* the organ of the Dutch Center until 1959, now appears six times a year with articles in English and French; its aim is to help Catholic research workers scientifically and to make the presence of Catholics felt in the sociological world. We must also mention the important scientific publication, *Archives de Sociologie des Religions,* published by the French national center of scientific research. The journal of the American Catholic Sociological Society has become a journal of religious sociology entitled *Sociological Analysis.* Lastly, in Italy there is Professor Acquaviva, who edits *Sociologia Religiosa,* which appears two or three times per year.

V

Protestant Religious Sociology

It would be unfair to condense within so small a space the great work done by the Protestants, and we shall only mention a small part of it. Our International Conference of Religious Sociology corresponds to their Colloque Européen de Sociologie du Protestantisme (European Congress of Protestant Sociology), which takes place every other year. Apart, however, from The Netherlands and some French publications, Protestant studies in Europe have been less concerned with pastoral work. The situation is slightly different in the United States. The Institute for Social and Religious Research was founded in 1922. It had been preceded in 1912 and 1919 by some extensive reports of the Federal Council of Churches on the relations between religion and the modern world. It disbanded in 1934 during the economic depression, but was revived later as the Bureau of Research and Survey of the National Council of Christian Churches in New York. While the first reports and studies were directed to the general reorientation of pastoral activity, other needs came to light between the two wars, which turned more to planning problems. Thus, a Congress was held in 1959 in Indianapolis on "Personnel Needs in Church Planning and Research". It was particularly concerned with the research necessary in order to organize various projects (Church establishments, training programs, financial campaigns, etc.).

American Protestants were not the only ones to undertake this project. In 1950 the World Council of Churches organized a meeting of theologians and sociologists in Geneva to study the importance of sociology for pastoral planning.[12]

We must also mention an important and more recent study, commissioned by the Church of England, on a general reassessment of the means available for its task.[13]

[12] See J. Ellul, "Kerkelijke Strategie en Sociologie," in *Sociologisch Bulletin* 2 (1951), pp. 33-47.

[13] *The Deployment and Payment of the Clergy. A Report by Leslie Paul* (London, 1964, Church Information Service, Church House, Westminster, London, S.W.1) 312 pages, and an appendix.

Much has been done in Germany (see the special article on this country by Norbert Greinacher, p. 111). But what is probably the most systematic treatment of the problem has been undertaken in The Netherlands, parallel with the pioneer work done by the Dutch Catholics. There the Sociological Institute of the Netherlands Reformed Church, with its headquarters in Utrecht, has studied religious behavior, the social characteristics of the Protestant population, Church establishments, etc., much like the work done by the Catholic KSKI.

Finally, there are the studies inspired by the World Council of Churches. Among these, the work of Professor de Vries and Paul Abrecht on the Churches in a changing society is outstanding. At the moment, the Institute of Social Studies of The Hague, under the direction of Professor de Vries, collaborates on behalf of the World Council with FERES in a study of the educational, social and health projects of the Christian Churches in the developing countries.

For a brief bibliography, see Section B, p. 110, at the end of this article.

VI

CONCLUSIONS

As religious sociology develops, stimulated by present-day problems, a dialogue is needed, not only by those working in the pastoral field, but also by theologians. A number of studies already tend in this direction.

No doubt, sociologists should be aware of their limits. But theologians, too, should make an effort. In particular, they should be able to understand the language and frame of mind that characterize the positive sciences, especially the human sciences, so that a dialogue becomes possible. These sciences are based on systematic observation and the inductive method. During the discussion of Schema 13 on the Church in the World, the Council debates showed how difficult it is for churchmen to adopt such a line, trained as they are in purely theological disciplines.

Such a change of attitude, obviously, cannot be brought about by sleight of hand. Psychological and sociological observation shows in any case that this level of communication can only be achieved after much groping and hesitation.

If religious, and particularly Catholic, sociology is still in its infancy, it is obvious that a genuine pastoral sociology has not yet been worked out. One may, however, hope for a quick start in the post-conciliar Church on condition that we have enough qualified men at our disposal.

In order to clarify still further what this new effort implies in the Church, this article is supplemented by articles on the work in some selected and very different countries: Germany, Belgium, Spain and Italy. A general bibliography, followed by a bibliography for the continents and countries that have not been studied in this article, may be found on pp. 141-144.

BIBLIOGRAPHICAL SUPPLEMENT—SECTION A

I GENERAL ORGANIZATION OF THE CHURCH

Canaletti-Gaudenti, A. *La statistica ad uso della Chiesa.* Rome: AVE, 1948.

Colson, J. *Les fonctions ecclésiales aux deux premiers siècles.* Paris: Desclée de Brouwer, 1956.

Chapin, F. S. "The Optimum Size of Institutions," in *American Journal of Sociology* 62 (1957), pp. 449-60.

Douglass, T. B. "Ecological Changes and the Church," in *Annals* 332 (1961), pp. 80-8.

Ellul, J. "Kerkelijke strategie en Sociologie," in *Sociologisch Bulletin* 5 (1951), pp. 33-64.

Fürstenberg, F. "Kirchenform und Gesellschafts-struktur," in *Sociologisch Bulletin* 14 (1960), pp. 100-13.

Houtart, F. "Les structures de l'Eglise," in *La Revue Nouvelle* 30 (1959), pp. 547-58.

Moulin, L. "Les formes du gouvernement local et provincial dans les ordres religieux," in *Revue Internationale des sciences administratives,* 1955.

Schmitt, T. J. *L'organisation ecclésiastique et la pratique religieuse dans l'archidiaconé d'Autun de 1650 à 1750.* Autun: Marcelin, 1957.

II THE PARISH

Azzali, L. *L'indagine sociologica di una parrocchia.* Cremona: Pizzorni, 1954.

Boulard, F. *L'étude d'une paroisse rurale.* Voiron: SAGMA, 1956.

Centre de recherches socio-religieuses. *Etude socio-religieuse de la paroisse du Béguinage.* Brussels: CRSR.

Daniel, Y. *L'Equipement paroissial de deux arrondissements parisiens* (Paroisses urbaines, paroisses rurales). Tournai: Casterman, 1958, pp. 28-43.

Donovan, J. D. *The Social Structure of the Parish, Sociology of the Parish.* Milwaukee: Bruce, 1951.

Fichter, J. H. *Social Relations in the Urban Parish.* University of Chicago, 1954.

Greeley, A. M. "Some Aspects of Interaction between Religious Groups in an Upper-Middle Class Roman Catholic Parish," in *Social Compass* 9 (1964), pp. 39-61.

Greinacher, N. *Die religionssoziologische Untersuchung der Pfarrei.* Freiburg, 1955.

Houtart, F. "Sociologie de la Paroisse comme assemblée eucharistique," in *Social Compass* 1 (1963), pp. 75-91.

Lebret, L. J. "Comment acquérir la connaissance sociologique d'une paroisse?" in *Structures sociales et pastorale paroissiale* (1948), pp. 29-40.

Milani, A. "La Parrocchia nella realità del quartiere," in *Orientamenti Sociali* 16 (1960), pp. 386-89.

Pin, E. "Can the Urban Parish Be a Community?" in *Gregorianum* 41 (1960), pp. 393-423.

Sokolsky, A. "Méthode de planning paroissial urbain," in *Social Compass* 7 (1960), pp. 313-24.

Virton, P. *Enquètes de sociologie paroissiale.* Paris: Spes, 1953.

Ward, C. *Priests and People.* University of Liverpool, 1961.

III COMPREHENSIVE PASTORAL WORK

Dingemans, L. "Les techniques du planning au service de la pastorale," in *Evangeliser* 13, pp. 34-43.

Dingemans, L., Houtart, F. *Pastorale d'une région industrielle.* Brussels: Ed. du CEP, 1964.

Houtart, C. *L'Eglise et la Pastorale des grandes villes.* Brussels: La Pensée catholique, 1956.

Klaine, R. *Planning paroissial et pastorale.* Lyons: Institut de Sociologie, 1957.

IV DISTRIBUTION OF THE CLERGY

Boulard, F. *Essor ou déclin du clergé francais?* Paris: Ed. du Cerf, 1950.

Dellepoort, J., Greinacher, N., Menges, W. *Die Deutsche Priesterfrage.* Mainz: Matthias Grünewald, 1961.

Hamelin, L. E. "Evolution numérique séculaire du clergé catholique dans le Québec," in *Recherches sociographiques* 2, pp. 189-242.

V CATHOLIC ACTION

Bourmont, R. P., Gueneau, C. "Un résultat d'enquête: vocations religieuses et mouvements féminins d'Action Catholique spécialisée," in *Supplément de la Vie Spirituelle* 12 (1959), pp. 27-63.

Dominguez, O. *El Campesino chileno y la Acción Catolica Rural.* Bogota: FERES, 1961.

VI THE SOCIAL FUNCTION OF CLERGY AND RELIGIOUS

1. CLERGY

Burchard, W. W. "Role Conflicts of Military Chaplains," in *American Sociological Review* (1954), pp. 528-35.

Burgalassi, S. *La vocazione ed il clero in Italia.* Vienna: Actes du colloque international, 1958, pp. 194-211.

Duocastella, R. *Problemas sacerdotales en España.* Madrid: Centro de Estudios de Sociologia Applicada, 1959.

Fichter, J. H. *Religion as an Occupation.* University of Notre Dame, 1961.

Gustafson, J. M. "An Analysis of the Problems of the Roles of the Minister," in *Journal of Religion* 34 (1954), pp. 187-91.

Houtart, F. "Le rôle du prêtre dans le monde moderne," in *Collectanea* (July-August, 1964).

James, E. O. *The Nature and Function of the Priesthood.* New York: Vanguard, 1955.

Kerkhofs, J. "Aspects sociologiques du sacerdoce," in *Nouvelle revue theologique* 82 (1960), pp. 289-99.

Perez, G. *El problema sacerdotal en América Latina.* Bogota: FERES, 1961.

Woolgar, M. J. *The Development of the Anglican and Roman Catholic Clergy as a Profession since the XVIII Century.* Leicester, 1961.

2. RELIGIOUS (MALE AND FEMALE)

Collard, E. *L'étude sociologique des communautés religieuses féminines et leur recrutement* (Vocation de la Sociologie et Sociologie des Vocations). Tournai: Casterman, 1958.

Dingemans, L. *Un siècle de développement des instituts religieux masculins en Belgique.* Brussels: CRSR, 1957.

Goddijn, H. P. "The Sociology of Religious Orders and Congregations," in *Social Compass* 7 (1960), pp. 431-77.

Szabo, D. "Essai sur quelques aspects sociologiques de la crise du recrutement sacerdotal en France," in *Bulletin de l'Institut de Recherche Economique et Sociologique* 24 (1958), pp. 635-46.

Vollmer, H. M. "Member Commitment and Organizational Competence in Religious Orders," in *Society & Institutions.* Berkeley publications, 1957, pp. 13-26.

3. VOCATIONS

McMahon, M. "Les jeunes-filles et la vocation religieuse: une enquête américaine," in *Lumen Vitae* 12 (1957), pp. 339-54.

——— *Vocation de la Sociologie et Sociologie des Vocations.* Tournai: Casterman, 1958.

4. LAITY

Schuyler, J. B. "The Role of the Laity in the Catholic Church," in *American Catholic Sociological Review* 20 (1959), pp. 290-307.

VII THE RELIGIOUS CONDITION OF THE PEOPLE

1. RELIGIOUS BEHAVIOR AND PRACTICES

Chombart de Lauwe, P. *La Pratique religieuse dominicale* (étude méthodologique). Paris: Centre de Documentation Universitaire, 1954.

Delcourt, M. "Valeur sociale d'un rite religieux: la première communion collective," in *Diogène* 36 (1961), pp. 83-92.

De Volder, N. "Inquiries into the Religious Life of Catholic Intellectuals," in *Journal of Social Psychology* 28 (1948), pp. 39-56.

Dingemans, L., Remy, J. *Charleroi et son agglomération* (aspects sociologiques de la pratique religieuse). Brussels: CRSR, 1962.

Dumont, F. *Eléments pour une psycho-sociologie de la prière*. Sarmel, 1958, pp. 115-27.

Gonzales, C. M. *El complimento pasqual en la dioceses de Bilbao*. Bilbao, 1954.

Hedemark, I. "Religious adfaerd: Danmark (Le comportement religieux au Danemark)," in *Sociologiske Meddelelser* 2 (1953), pp. 25-33.

Raffard, H. "Résultats de l'enquête de sociologie religieuse du 21 nov. 1953 à Casablanca," in *Faits et Idées* 29 (1955), pp. 24-9.

Schmitt-Eglin, P. *Le mécanisme de la déchristianisation* (recherche pastorale sur le peuple des campagnes). Paris: Alsatia, 1952.

Toldo, A. *Risultati dell'inchiesta sulla frequenza alla messa festiva nel comune di Bologna*. Bologna: ISAB, 1960.

Verscheure, J., Deproster, E., Traulle, C. *Aspects sociologiques de la pratique dominicale* (diocese de Lille). Lille: CDESR, 1961.

2. RELIGIOUS ATTITUDES

(a) *In General:*

Carrier, H. "Le rôle des groupes de référence dans l'intégration des attitudes religieuses," in *Social Compass* 7 (1960), pp. 134-60.

Dynos, R. R. *The Relations of Community Characteristics to Religious Organizations and Behavior* (Community Structure and Analysis). New York, 1951.

Isambert, F. A. "L'analyse des attitudes religieuses," in *Archives de Sociologie des Religions* 11 (1961), pp. 35-51.

Maitre, J. "Un sondage polonais sur les attitudes religieuses de la jeunesse," in *Archives de Sociologie des Religions* 12 (1961), pp. 133-43.

(b) *Rural Environment:*

Boulard, F. *Problèmes missionaires de la France rurale*. Paris: Ed. du Cerf, 1955.

D'Ascenzi, G. "La situazione religiosa nelle campagne italiane," in *Orientamenti social* 11, pp. 426-32.

Laloux, J. *Problèmes actuels du monde rural*. Brussels: La Pensée catholique, 1956.

Mendras, H. *Etudes de la société rurale*. Paris: Colin, 1953.

Nuesse, C. J. "Membership Trends in a Rural Catholic Parish," in *Rural Sociology* 22 (1957), pp. 123-30.

(c) *Urban environment:*

Del Valle, F. "Homos perdido la clase obrera en España?" in *Razon y Fe* 145, pp. 484-504; 597-611.

Dumont, J. *Résultat d'une enquête de mentalité ouvrière à Liège et à Charleroi*. Brussels: CRSR, 1956.

Gemelli, A. "Quello che i lavoratori pensano di noi sacerdoti," in *Revista del Clero italiano* 23 (1942), pp. 305-9.

Smet, E. de. *La situation religieuse et morale de la classe ouvrière flamande* (Ontkerstening, herkenstening van de arbeiders). Antwerp: 't Groeit, 1950.

3. RELIGIOUS MOTIVATATION

Braden, C. S. "Why People Are Religious," in *Journal of Bible and Religion* 15 (1947), pp. 38-45.

Lenski, G. "Some Social Correlates of Religious Interest," in *Review of Religious Research* 1 (1953), pp. 24-9.

Pin, E. *Elementos para una sociologia del catolicismo latino-americano.* Bogota: FERES, 1963.

Schuyler, B. "Religious Behavior in Northern Parish: a study of motivating values," in *American Catholic Sociological Review* 19 (1958), pp. 134-44.

4. RELIGIOUS PATHOLOGY

Briggs, L. P. "The Syncretism of Religion in S. E. Asia," in *Journal of the American Oriental Society* 17, pp. 230-49.

Kraemer, H. "Syncretism as a Religious and Missionary Problem," in *International Review of Missions* 43 (1954), pp. 253-73.

Messinger, J. C. "Reinterpretation of Christian and Indigenous Belief in a Nigerian Nativist Church," in *American Anthropologist* 62 (1960), pp. 268-78.

Pereira de Quiroz, M. *La guerre sainte au Brésil: le mouvement messianique du "Contistado."* São Paulo, 1957.

Procopio de Camarargo, C. *Aspectos sociologicos del Espiritismo en São Paulo.* Bogota: FERES, 1961.

Thompson, D. E. *Maya Paganism and Christianity: a historical fusion of two religions.* New Orleans: Middle Amercan Research Institute, 1952.

VIII SOCIAL CONDITION OF CATHOLIC POPULATIONS

Doorn, J. A. "De emancipatie der Nederlandse Roomskatholiek in de sociologische Literatuur," in *Sociologische Gids* 5 (1958), pp. 196-204.

Godefroy, J., Thoen, C. "Criminaliteit en moraliteit onder Katholieken," in *Social Compass* 1 (1953), pp. 1-12.

Greinacher, N. "Die Familie in der Katholischen Pfarrgemeinde," in *Wörterbuch der Politik* 8 (1959), pp. 347-49.

Thomas, J. L. *The American Catholic Family.* Englewood Cliffs, New Jersey: Prentice Hall, 1956.

Troude, R. "Le niveau moral de la Normandie selon quatre critères statistiques," in *Etudes normandes* 26 (1958), pp. 1-11.

Vogt, E. Z., Dea, D. "A comparative study of the role of values in social action in two S.W. communities," in *American Sociological Review* 18 (1953), pp. 645-54.

IX PASTORAL ACTIVITY

1. VARIOUS TYPES OF ACTIVITY

Chelini, J. *La ville et l'Eglise.* Paris: Ed. du Cerf, 1958.

Greeley, A. M. *The Church and the Suburbs.* New York: Sheed & Ward, 1959.

Labbens, J. *L'Eglise et les Centres urbains.* Paris: Spes, 1959.

Lee, R. (ed.) *Cities and Churches: readings on the urban church.* Philadelphia: Westminster Press, 1962.

Laloux, J. *Mettre l'Eglise en Etat de mission.* Brussels: CEP, 1964.

Winninger, P. *Construire des églises: les dimensions des paroisses et les contradictions de l'apostolat dans les villes.* Paris: Ed. du Cerf, 1957.

———— *Paroisses urbaines, paroisses rurales* (Vᵉ Conference intern. de sociologie religieuse). Paris: Casterman, 1958.

———— *Las tareas de la iglesia en america latina.* Bogota: FERES, 1964.

2. LITURGY

Bergendoff, C. "What governs and shapes liturgical development," in *Ecumenical Review* 7 (1955), pp. 353-58.

Berger, P. L. *The Noise of Solemn Assemblies.* New York: Doubleday, 1961.

Häring, B. "Mentalité technique et accès à l'univers liturgique," in *Lumen Vitae* 13 (1958), pp. 655-64.

Herlin, O. "Liturgy and Society," in *Acta sociologica* 3 (1958), pp. 91-7.

LeBras, G. "Liturgie et sociologie," in *Revue des sciences religieuses* (1956), pp. 291-304.

Schreuder, O. "Religious attitudes, group-consciousness, liturgy and education," in *Social Compass* X/1 (1963), pp. 29-52.

3. COMMUNICATION CHANNELS

Parker, E. C., Barry, D. W., Smythe, D. W. *The Television Audience and Religion.* New York: Harper, 1955.

Wolseley, R. E. "The Influence of the Religious Press," in *Religion in Life* 26 (1956), pp. 75-80.

4. MISSIONS (TO CATHOLICS AND NON-CHRISTIANS)

Luzbetak, L. J. *The Church and Cultures: An Applied Missionary Anthropology.* Techny, Illinois: Divine Word Publications, 1963.

Korb, G. M. *The Scientific Screening of Missionary Methods.* Washington, 1961.

Motte, J. F., Dourmad, M. *Mission générale, oeuvre d'Eglise.* Paris: Ed. du Cerf, 1957.

X CHRISTIAN SECULAR ACTIVITY

1. SOCIAL AND CULTURAL ACTION

Rezsohazy, R. "Autour du catholicisme social en Belgique," in *Revue Nouvelle* (1959), pp. 217-23.

Spencer, S. W. "Religious and Spiritual Values in Social Casework Practice," in *Social Casework* 38 (1951), pp. 519-24.

Torres, C., Corredor, B. *Las escuelas radiofonicas de Sutatenza, Colombia: evaluación sociologica de los resultados.* Bogota: FERES, 1960.

2. CATHOLIC SCHOOLS

Brothers, J. *Church and School.* University of Liverpool, 1964.

Fichter, J. H. *Parochial School.* University of Notre Dame, 1958.

Godefroy, J. "De toekomstige Behoefte aan Docenten bij Het Katholiek Onderwijs in Nederland," in *Social Compass* 2 (1954), pp. 168-82.

Mehok, W. J. "Survey of Jesuit High Schools: Evaluation 1946-52," in *Jesuit Educational Quarterly* 14 (1952), pp. 204-18.

Rossi, P., Rossi, A. S. "Background and Consequences of Parochial School Education," in *Harvard Educational Review* 27 (1957), pp. 168-99.

BIBLIOGRAPHICAL SUPPLEMENT—SECTION B

Abrecht, P. *The Churches and Rapid Social Change.* New York: Doubleday, 1961.

Banning, W. *Handboek Pastorale Sociologie.* (4 Vols.) The Hague, 1953-57.

Bissing, W. von. "Die Evangelische Predicht in der modernen industrielgesellschaft," in *Zeitschrift für Evangelische Ethik* 2 (1961), pp. 105-14.

Dahm, K. W. "Die soziologische Stellung des Pfarrers in der heutigen Gesellschaft," in *Evangelische Akademie, Rheinland, Westfalen 9,* pp. 14-25.

Dynes, R. R. *Mobile Industrial Workers and the Church: a Study of People on the Move in Ohio's Atomic Area.* National Council of Churches, Division of Home Missions.

Jordan, R. H. "Social Functions of the Churches in Oaksville," in *Sociological and Social Research* 40, pp. 107-11.

Rendtorff, T. *Die soziale Struktur der Gemeinde.* Hamburg, 1958.

Matthes, J. "Ideologische Züge in der neueren evangelischen Sozialarbeit," in *Lutheran World* 7 (1960), pp. 23-45.

Norbert Greinacher/ *Essen, W. Germany*

Pastoral Sociology in Germany and Austria Since 1945

Becausе of the pioneer work of Max Weber (1864-1920) we can already speak of a certain tradition in religious sociology in Germany. The Church, however, showed no interest in this work or even looked upon it with mistrust. Apart from a few exceptions, no attention was paid to problems of pastoral sociology until after 1945.

Let us look first at the more important institutions that concerned themselves with these problems. After the war, the Catholic International Institute for Refugee Problems (Katholische internationale soziologische Institut für Flüchtlingsfragen) was founded, and in 1952 Walter Menges gave it its present name of Catholic Institute of Social Research (Katholisches Institut für Sozial-Forschung). Although this Institute busied itself at first with refugee problems, it has turned its attention in recent years particularly to investigations in various towns and regions. These investigations, which were concerned with attendance at the Sunday service, helped in the preparation for regional missions. Special mention should be made here of the investigations that took place in Limburg and Munich.[1]

---

* NORBERT GREINACHER: Born April 26, 1931 in Freiburg, W. Germany, he was ordained in 1956 for the Diocese of Freiburg. He studied at the University of Freiburg, the Institut Catholique in Paris and at the University of Vienna, earning his doctorate in theology in 1955.

[1] Walter Menges, *Soziale Verhältnisse und kirchliches Verhalten im*

The year 1958 saw the foundation of the Pastoral Sociological Institute of the Archdiocese of Paderborn and the Diocese of Essen (Pastoralsoziologische Institut des Erzbistums Paderborn und des Bistums Essen), until 1963 under the direction of Norbert Greinacher. Today its director is Egon Golomb, and it is now known as the Social Institute of the Diocese of Essen; Department of Ecclesiastical Social Research (Sozialinstitut des Bistums Essen, Abteilung kirchliche Sozialforschung). This institute also undertook research into Sunday mass-attendance.[2] Mention must also be made of research into the religious attitude of young people, attendance at mass of the sailors in the harbor of Duisburg, the clergy and the new generation of priests, as well as of an unfinished inquiry into the religious situation in the industrial community.

These two institutes belong to the International Federation of Institutes of Catholic Social Research (FERES), which has its headquarters in Brussels. These are the only two institutes in Germany that have specialized in pastoral sociological research. But there are also various institutions that show great interest in this kind of research and have in some measure taken part in it. This interest is mainly in attendance at mass on Sundays and prepares the groundwork for regional missions. Here we may point, for example, to the Institute for Christian Social Sciences (Institut für christliche Sozialwissenschaften) in Münster, to the report on ecclesiastical social research in the diocese of Fulda, a similar report on pastoral functions in Osnabrück, the work of the Redemptorist Fathers in Gars am Inn and investigations undertaken in connection with social seminars in the diocese of Mainz and in Speyer.

Church statistics are important for this research work. The Center for Church Statistics of Catholic Germany (Zentralstelle

---

Limburger Raum (Limburg, 1959); *idem,* "Soziale Schichtung und kirchliches Verhalten in der Groszstadt," in *Herder-Korrespondenz* 15 (1960), pp. 280-6. This Institute also undertook inquiries in other places, such as Trier, Mannheim, Ludwigshafen and Nuremberg-Fürth. The many reports published by the Institute give the results.

[2] Among other places, the reports are published in Essen, Dortmund, Bottrop, Gelsenkirchen, Karlsruhe, Marl, Wattenscheid, Duisburg.

für kirchliche Statistik des katholischen Deutschlands), under the direction of Franz Groner, collects statistical data about the Church's situation on the basis of a questionnaire sent out once a year to the parish priests. The results are published from time to time in the *Kirchliches Handbuch,* the last volume of which appeared in 1962 and covered the years 1957-1961.[3]

In the Evangelical Church there is, above all, the Institute of Christian Social Sciences (Institut für christliche Gesellschaftswissenschaften) in Münster, under the direction of Heinz Dietrich Wendland, and at the moment occupied with a rather extensive research project on the religious situation among the inhabitants of the German Federal Republic. The Bureau of Church Statistics of the German Evangelical Church (Kirchenstatistische Amt der Evangelischen Kirche in Deutschland) has published valuable statistical reports under the direction of Paul Zieger. In the study group on religious sociology of the German Sociological Association (Arbeitsgemeinschaft für Religionssoziologie innerhalb der deutschen Gesellschaft für Soziologie), there is fruitful collaboration among all kinds of students of religious sociology.

For Austria, we must mention first of all the Institute of Ecclesiastical Social Research (Institut für kirchliche Sozialforschung), which was founded in 1952 and is directed today by H. Bogensberger. It undertook a census of attendance at Church services (Innsbruck, Flagenfurt, Linz, Lienz, Vienna, Salzburg, St Pölten, and elsewhere), parochial and diocesan research, projects at parish level and of a wider scope. There is also the Center for Social Research (Sozialforschungstelle) of the diocese of Linz, under the direction of M. Lengauer and U. Suk, as well as a department for Church Statistics in the Austrian Institute of pastoral work. As far as we know, there is no institution in Switzerland that deals with pastoral sociological studies.

From the various institutions we may now pass to the more important publications. Pastoral sociological research obviously turned first to the investigation of Church communities. In 1955

[3] Franz Groner, ed., *Kirchliches Handbuch. Amtliches Jahrbuch der katholischen Kirche Deutschlands,* Vol. 25 (1957-1961, Cologne, 1962).

Norbert Greinacher published his *Soziologie der Pfarrei*, which surveyed the research done in Europe and laid down suggestions for the religious sociological investigation of a parish.[4] Erich Bodzenta made a comprehensive study of the social and religious situation of an industrial village in Austria.[5] In 1957 appeared the German translation of Joseph Fichter's work on the social structure of the urban parish, in which he attempted to establish a typological analysis of parishioners and to look at the parish in the light of its overall social environment.[6] The same author also gave us a study of the groups and organizations of a parish in Münster.[7] An important step forward in this study of parish communities was made by Osmund Schreuder, who applied Parson's sociological theory to the parish as a social organization.[8] The inner structure and sociological functions of a parish were dealt with in a study by J. Schasching.[9] From the sociological point of view, Egon Golomb contributed an important project for the reorientation of Church communities in a large town.[10] The same author published a good survey of parochial sociology in the Catholic sphere.[11] Erich Bodzenta made an attempt to classify parishes in the book, *Soziologie der Kirchengemeinde,* edited by D. Goldschmidt, H. Schelsky and F. Greiner. This study provides a sound insight into the sociological prob-

[4] *Soziologie der Pfarrei. Wege zur Untersuchung* (Colar-Freiburg, 1955).

[5] Erich Bodzenta, *Industriedorf im Wohlstand* (Mainz, 1962).

[6] Freiburg, 1957.

[7] *Soziologie der Pfarrgruppen. Untersuchungen zur Struktur und Dynamik der Gruppen einer deutschen Pfarrei* (Münster, 1958).

[8] *Kirche im Vorort. Soziologische Erkundung einer Pfarrei* (Freiburg-Basel-Vienna, 1962); *idem,* "Ein soziologischer Richtungsbegriff der Pfarrei," in *Social Compass* 6 (1959), pp. 177-203.

[9] Hugo Rahner, ed., *Soziologie der Pfarre* (Freiburg, 1956), pp. 97-124.

[10] Egon Golomb, "Seelsorgsplanung in der Groszstadt," in *Trierer Theologische Zeitschrift* 72 (1963), pp. 123-49. On the same subject, cf. Paul Winninger, *Pfarrgemeinde und Groszstadt. Die Ausdehnung der Pfarrei und die Grundsätze des Apostolates in der Städten* (Colar-Freiburg, 1959).

[11] Dietrich Goldschmidt and Joachim Matthes, eds., *Ergebnisse und Ansätze pfarrsoziologischer Bemühungen im katholischen Raum: Probleme der Religionssoziologie* (Cologne and Opladen, 1962), pp. 202-13.

lems of a parish.[12] On the evangelical side, mention must be made of the studies by Freytag, Köster and Rendtorff.[13]

A number of publications deal with regional and even wider studies of this kind. The work of Walter Menges, concerned with Limburg, has already been mentioned.[14] Alfons Weyand has published the results of a churchgoers' census in the industrial town of Marl.[15] A new work by Annemarie Burger has collected valuable material on social relationships in Germany as influenced by denominational factors.[16] Joseph Höffner deals with the situation of German Catholicism today.[17] Norbert Greinacher has traced the development of religious practice in Germany.[18] Erich Bodzenta has surveyed the social and religious situation in Austria,[19] while there are two studies of the situation of the Catholic Church in Europe.[20]

Another series of studies has turned to the subject of social classes and categories. Among these, H. O. Wölber has concen-

[12] Erich Bodzenta, "Zur sozial-religiösen Typologie der katholischen Pfarre," in *Soziologie der Kirchengemeinde,* Dietrich Goldschmidt, Helmut Schelsky and Franz Greiner, eds. (Stuttgart, 1960).

[13] J. Freytag, *Die Kirchengemeinde in soziologischer Sicht. Ziel und Weg empirischer Forschungen* (Hamburg, 1959); R. Köster, *Die Kirchentreuen. Erfahrungen und Ergebnisse einer soziologischen Untersuchung in einer evangelischen groszstädtischen Kirchengemeinde* (Stuttgart, 1959); Trutz Rendtorff, *Die soziale Struktur der Gemeinde. Die kirchlichen Lebensformen im gesellschaftlichen Wandel der Gegenwart. Eine soziologische Untersuchung* (Hamburg, 1958).

[14] See footnote 1.

[15] Alfons Weyand, *Formen religiöser Praxis in einem werdenden Industrieraum* (Münster, 1963); see also Linus Grond, "Die Kirche in einer internationalen Stadt (Genf)," in *Herder-Korrespondenz* 15 (1961), pp. 323-9.

[16] *Religionszugehörigkeit und soziales Verhalten. Untersuchungen und Statistiken der neueren Zeit in Deutschland* (Göttingen, 1964).

[17] "Der Deutsche Katholizismus in der pluralistischen Gesellschaft der Gegenwart," in *Jahrbuch des Instituts für christliche Sozialwissenschaften,* Vol. I (Münster, 1960), pp. 31-50.

[18] "Pastoralsoziologische Überlegungen zur Entwicklung der religiösen Praxis," in *Lebendige Seelsorge* 13 (1962), pp. 221-8.

[19] *Die Katholiken in Österreich* (Vienna, 1962).

[20] Linus Grond, "Der europäische Katholizismus. Einige statistischen und soziologischen Betrachtungen im Zusammenhang mit der europäischen Integration," in *Herder-Korrespondenz* 14 (1960), pp. 443-85; Shin C. Anzai, *Die religiöse Praxis der Katholiken im Zusammenhang mit einigen Sozialfaktoren in Mittel- und Westeuropa* (Diss.) (Vienna, 1961).

trated on the religious attitude of the young,[21] while Joseph
Höffner and Norbert Greinacher have tried to analyze the effects
of the industrial revolution on the religious attitude, particularly
of the working classes.[22] Gregor Siefer has given a careful sociological analysis of social relationships in the activities of worker-
priests.[23] Josef Laloux has studied the religious situation of the
agricultural population, though mainly referring to France.[24]
There is an interesting work by M. A. J. M. Matthejssen on the
relation of the Catholic intelligentsia to the Church in a European
context.[25] Two studies deal with pastoral problems arising out of
the social disintegration resulting from migration.[26] Sociological
and religious questions connected with leaving the Church and
conversion have been treated in a study by Norbert Greinacher.[27]

Several studies treat of the *clergy, secular and regular,* and
their recruitment. The German situation has been surveyed in a
work on the clerical problem in Germany: *Die deutsche Priesterfrage.*[28] The motives that may determine a man or boy to consider the priesthood have been examined by Crottogini and
Stenger and also appear as the results of an inquiry conducted

[21] *Religion ohne Entscheidung. Volkskirche am Beispiel der jungen Generation,* 2nd ed. (Göttingen, 1960).
[22] Joseph Höffner, *Industrielle Revolution und religiöse Krise. Schwund
und Wandel des religiösen Verhaltens in der modernen Gesellschaft*
(Cologne and Opladen, 1961); Norbert Greinacher, "Kirche und Ar-
beiterschaft," in *Oberrheinisches Pastoralblatt* 62 (1961), pp. 73-82.
[23] *Die Mission der Arbeiterpriester* (Essen, 1960).
[24] *Die religiöse Entwicklung auf dem Lande, soziologisch und seel-
sorgerlich betrachtet* (Munich, 1962); cf. Henri Mendras *et al.,* "Soziale
und religiöse Krise im französischen Bauerntum," in *Herder-Korrespondenz* 16 (1962), pp. 180-6.
[25] "Die katholische Intelligenz im neuen Europa," in *Herder-Korrespondenz* 15 (1961), pp. 375-81.
[26] "Soziologische Beobachtungen von der europäischen Völkerwander-
ung," in *Herder-Korrespondenz* 16 (1962), pp. 373-9 and 17 (1963), pp.
326-32.
[27] "Die Entwicklung der Kirchenaustritte und Kirchenübertritte und
ihre Ursachen," in *Kirchliches Handbuch* 25 (Cologne, 1962), pp. 441-52.
[28] J. J. Dellepoort, N. Greinacher, W. Menges, *Die deutsche Priesterfrage. Eine soziologische Untersuchung über Klerus und Priesternach-
wuchs in Deutschland* (Mainz, 1961); cf. Franz Groner, "Statistik des
Klosternachwuchses in Deutschland," in *Kölner, Aachener und Essener
Pastoralblatt* 11 (1959), pp. 183-92; *idem,* "Der Weltpriesternachwuchs
in Deutschland statistisch gesehen," *ibid.,* pp. 62-9.

in Vienna.[29] There is also an evangelical study on the position of the minister in modern society.[30] The situation in Austria has been surveyed by J. J. Dellepoort and L. Grond.[31] H. Ehringer has thrown some light on the recruitment problems in orders of women in Austria.[32] And a book on the problem of the priestly vocation in Europe, *Die europäische Priesterfrage,* provides a general impression.[33]

So far, we have concentrated on empirical studies, and we may now turn to the theoretical questions that have risen in this field. Fernand Boulard, whose guide to pastoral sociology, *Wegweiser in die Pastoralsoziologie,* was translated into German,[34] provides a good introduction. Pol Virton's sociological reflections of a parish priest, *Soziologische Betrachtungen eines Seelsorgers,* was also translated from the French.[35] In his book on pastoral work in a new world, *Seelsorge in einer neuen Welt,* Victor Schurr devotes a chapter to pastoral sociology.[36]

Sociologists are naturally concerned with the *social aspect of the Church in contemporary society.* The principles have been dealt with in a remarkable essay, "Ist die Dauerreflektion institutionalisierbar? Zum Thema einer modernen Religionssoziologie" [37] by Helmut Schelsky, on whether the permanent aspect of the Church is compatible with its institutional aspect. On this

[29] J. Crottogini, *Werden und Krise des Priesterberufes* (Einsiedeln-Zürich-Cologne, 1955); Hermann Stenger, *Wissenschaft und Zeugnis. Die Ausbildung des katholischen Seelsorgeklerus in psychologischer Sicht* (Salzburg, 1961); T. Lindner, L. Lentner and A. Holl, *Priesterbild und Berufswahlmotive. Ergebnisse einer sozialpsychologischen Untersuchung bei den Wiener Mittelschülern* (Vienna, 1963).

[30] G. Wurzbacher *et al., Der Pfarrer in der modernen Gesellschaft* (Hamburg, 1960).

[31] "Stand und Bedarf an Priestern in Österreich," in *Social Compass* 4 (1957), pp. 108-48; cf. Egon Golomb, *Die steirische Priesterschaft. Eine empirisch-soziologische Untersuchung* (Diss.) (Graz, 1959).

[32] *Die weiblichen Orden in Österreich* (Diss.) (Vienna, 1962).

[33] F. Jachym and J. J. Dellepoort, *Die europäische Priesterfrage* (Vienna, 1959).

[34] Munich, 1960.

[35] Munich, 1962.

[36] Salzburg, 1957, pp. 109-35; cf. K. Gémes, *Die Soziologie im Dienste der Seelsorge* (Diss.) (Graz, 1956).

[37] *Zeitschrift für evangelische Ethik* 1 (1957), pp. 153-74. For further discussion of this article, see *ibid.,* 1 (1957), pp. 254-90 and 3 (1959), pp. 193-220.

point the evangelical studies by Matthes and Wendland must also be mentioned.[38] H. P. Desqueyrat has analyzed the present religious situation in relation to the Church's effectiveness.[39] The problem of the Church in an industrial society has been dealt with by J. Schasching,[40] while the social change in the life of the Church was studied in the two well-known works by Klemens Brockmüller.[41] Although more in the nature of a pamphlet, Carl Amery's study of German Catholicism has been widely discussed.[42] Several authors are concerned with the urgent problem of the transition from a national Church to some other form in our pluralistic society.[43]

Two studies tackle the question of the social limitations and conditioning of Catholic teaching on morals and society. Of these, Schöllgen deals with the principles, while Knoll has a rather polemical slant.[44]

Finally, a few studies treat of the *Church as a social institution* from the sociological point of view. Among these we must first mention the work done by W. and H. P. M. Goddijn,[45] as well as a contribution made by Norbert Greinacher.[46] There are also valuable indications in the report of the International Conference

[38] Joachim Matthes, *Die Emigration der Kirche aus der Gesellschaft* (Hamburg, 1964). Heinz Dietrich Wendland, *Die Kirche in der modernen Gesellschaft* (Hamburg, 1958).

[39] *Zur religiösen Krise der Gegenwart* (Munich, 1961).

[40] *Kirche und industrielle Gesellschaft* (Vienna, 1960).

[41] *Christentum am Morgen des Atomzeitalters* (Frankfurt, 1954); *Industriekultur und Religion* (Frankfurt, 1964).

[42] *Die Kapitulation oder der deutsche Katholizismus heute* (Hamburg, 1963).

[43] Rudolf Hernegger, *Volkskirche oder Kirche der Gläubigen?* (Nuremberg, 1959); *idem, Macht ohne Auftrag* (Olten-Freiburg, 1963). Peter L. Berger, *Kirche ohne Auftrag* (Stuttgart, 1962); Georg F. Vicedom, *Das Dilemma der Volkskirche. Gedanken und Erwägungen* (Munich, 1961); E. Stammler, *Protestanten ohne Kirche* (Stuttgart, 1960).

[44] Werner Schöllgen, "Die soziologischen Grundlagen der katholischen Sittenlehre," in Fritz Tillman's *Handbuch der katholischen Sittenlehre,* Vol. 5 (Düsseldorf, 1953); Albert Maria Knoll, *Katholische Kirche und scholastisches Naturrecht* (Vienna, 1962).

[45] *Kirche als Institution. Einführung in die Religionssoziologie* (Mainz, 1963).

[46] "Soziologische Aspekte des Selbstvollzuges der Kirche," in *Handbuch für Pastoraltheologie,* Vol. 1 (Freiburg, 1964).

of Religious Sociology on *Who Belongs to the Church?*[47] Bernard Häring contributes a comprehensive study of the interrelationship between religion and the Church on the one hand, and society on the other.[48]

In spite of the impressive list of publications on pastoral sociological problems, we must state that pastoral theology is still in its infancy. One would wish that it were not merely a matter of collecting empirical facts. At the very start of the inquiry, and certainly when it comes to the assessment and interpretation of the results, one should be guided by scientific hypotheses. Without such a guide one is bound to get lost in a jungle of figures. Above all, one must constantly ask the question what empirical facts, such as a census of churchgoers, are supposed to mean. In other words, one should try to inquire into the motives and religious attitudes that determine the religious situation. A further difficulty lies in the translation of pastoral sociological data into pastoral practice. Here one misses a close cooperation between pastoral sociologists and pastoral theologians. It is true that sociologists can certainly make an important contribution to the problem of the sociological image of the Church in a changed world and to the sociological determination of the Church's self-awareness, but on this point there is but little progress to report. The whole field that Karl Rahner once tried to mark off for theological and religious sociology is still largely a virgin field. By this he meant that theological reflection should turn to the scientific results of religious sociology. In this context belongs, for instance, the question of what the meaning is of the "un-Churching" and secularization that we observe around us in the total prospect of salvation history.

In this direction, pastoral sociology has made a hopeful beginning, but there is still much to be done that is of the greatest importance for the Church if we wish to produce genuine and reliable norms for our pastoral work.

[47] Walter Menges and Norbert Greinacher, eds., *Die Zugehörigkeit zur Kirche* (Mainz, 1964).

[48] *Macht und Ohnmacht der Religion. Religionssoziologie als Anruf,* 2nd ed. (Salzburg, 1956).

Jean Remy / *Brussels, Belgium*

Religious Sociology in Belgium

Belgian research in the field of religious sociology was mainly inspired by pastoral needs. The first requirement was to take stock of the de-christianization that prevailed in the various parts of the country. Abbé Collard, therefore, organized a nationwide inquiry that allowed him to draw a map of the state of religious practice throughout the country; this clearly showed the de-christianized regions. A summary of this work appeared in the periodical *Lumen Vitae*.[1] This summary produced a shock in different sections of society, even among socialist politicians. Mr. Evalenka, of the Free University of Brussels, then compared the data provided by this map with the voting results of the political elections.

On the other hand, François Houtart studied the problem of parochial structures in relation to their adaptation to the surrounding religious situation. On this basis he launched a second line of research with contemporary society in mind, leading to the adaptation that this society required of the Church. At first,

---

* JEAN REMY: Born November 14, 1928 in Soumagne, Belgium. He studied at the University of Louvain, earning degrees in philosophy in 1954, political and social sciences in 1956, economic sciences in 1959, and receiving, in 1960, the prize of the "Comité de Défense de l'Epargne mobilière".

[1] *Lumen Vitae*, VII, No. 4 (1952).

this research was directed to the question of parish boundaries,[2] but this question led gradually to the study of more fundamental problems.[3]

Most studies of both kinds developed either within the framework of Louvain University or within that of the Center for Socio-Religious Research in Brussels. In this Center a number of studies were inspired by the regional missions. These missions were not conceived merely as periods of intensive preaching but included a reassessment of pastoral procedure, an important preliminary step toward research. Thus, sociological research became useful in that it clarified the profound changes that had taken place in a given region and the problems they created for pastoral work. These investigations did not simply formulate the questions that the contemporary world wants to put to the Church. They often included an examination of the Catholic situation in a region and particularly of religious practice there.

Having indicated the main lines and the main centers of this research work, we can briefly turn to some of the work done in the two fields mentioned above.

Insofar as the inquiries into religious practice are concerned, Jan Kerkhofs has analyzed Belgian Limburg and shown that dechristianization there was not caused by the industrialization of the region.[4] A study of religious practice in the urban district of Charleroi[5] tackled the problem of Catholics attending mass outside their parish church, apart from all those other special problems implied by an inquiry of this kind. The phenomenon was considered important because it affects one-third of the male adults, and because it is linked to the fitness and geographical

[2] "Structures sociales et circonscriptions religieuses," in *Lumen Vitae,* VI, Nos. 1 and 2 (Brussels, 1951), pp. 221-31.

[3] "Faut-il abandonner la paroisse dans la ville moderne?" in *Nouvelle Revue Théologique* (Louvain, 1960), pp. 602-13.

[4] J. Kerkhofs, "Godsdienst praktijk en sociaal milieu. Proeve van godsdienst-sociologische studie der provincie Limburg," in *Cahiers de Lumen Vitae,* V (Brussels, 1953), 377 pages.

[5] L. Dingemans and J. Remy, *Charleroi et son agglomération: Aspects sociologiques de la pratique religieuse* (Brussels, Centre de Recherches Socio-Religieuses, 1962), 400 pages.

mobility of the households. Other studies have been made of urban districts, such as Paul Minon's work on Liège,[6] J. Van Houtte's on Ghent[7] and J. Laloux's on Seraing.[8] Apart from these studies, mainly concerned with industrial and urban districts, mention must be made of the inquiries into religious practice, especially in rural districts, conducted by Laloux.[9] Here a distinction was seen to operate between those who earn their livelihood locally and those whose work demands constant traveling.

In the type of research launched by Houtart, study has mainly concentrated on the changes that various regions have undergone and on the causes leading to these changes. In this field, one may point to a study of the urban district of Charleroi, which also contains a historical analysis.[10] There has also appeared a sociological analysis-in-depth of the urban area of Seraing.[11] This analysis tries to pinpoint the attitudes and behavior of those who are committed, Christians and priests, in face of the prevailing social values and standards in the region. Here one might also refer to various contributions made by Houtart in connection with the problems created for pastoral work by an urban environment.

These analytical studies begin gradually to clarify the part a sociologist can play in suggesting new directives for action. The first conclusions in this field were published in 1964. They may be found, for instance, in a section of Laloux's work on Seraing. Dingemans and Houtart have just published their *Pastorale d'une région industrielle*,[12] which gives the result of their investigation

[6] P. Minon, *Le peuple liègeois; structures sociales et attitudes religieuses* (Liège, 1955).

[7] J. Van Houtte, *De mispraktijk in de Gentse agglomeratie. Misonderzoek en sociologische interpretatie* (Louvain, Catholic University, 1963).

[8] J. Laloux, *Mettre l'Eglise en état de mission* (Brussels, Les Editions du Cep, 1964).

[9] J. Laloux, *Evolution religieuse du milieu rural* (Gembloux, Duculot).

[10] J. Remy, *Charleroi et son agglomération; Unités de vie sociales, structures socio-économiques;* A. Delobelle, *Charleroi et son agglomération: Analyse de sociologie historique.*

[11] J. Laloux, *op. cit.*

[12] L. Dingemans and F. Houtart, *Pastorale d'une région industrielle* (Brussels: Les Editions du Cep, 1964).

and indicates the direction to be taken on the basis of an analysis made of the urban area of Charleroi. In the same way, the clergy of Liège have asked that a sociological adviser be nominated to the various commissions set up to sort out pastoral problems.

Apart from these pastoral suggestions, there have even been a certain number of meetings to ensure a dialogue between theologians and sociologists. In December, 1963, there was such a meeting at Namur between professors of theology and religious sociologists. But many informal contacts have been established as well. Their influence is clearly visible in such studies as that of Laloux on Seraing.

From the analytic research work, which was essentially sociological at the start, the need arose for studies of greater depth and quality. In some cases, enough research results have accumulated to justify a more direct contribution when it comes to working out pastoral directives. But this is only a first phase where we ought not to stop.

New basic studies are required to produce more definite solutions to some concrete pastoral problems. On this point, the incorporation of the Center of Socio-Religious Research with the University of Louvain in October, 1964, will prove an advantage. Among the topics that demand a thorough and systematic treatment there are particularly the interrelationship between religion and industrial society, and the role of the priest in the contemporary world.

Rogelio Duocastella / *Barcelona, Spain*

Sociology and Pastoral Theology in Spain

It is generally true that religious sociology is a young science, but in Spain it is even younger. Although we can date its beginnings before 1936, it was not until after the Civil War that it experienced any real promise. Except for a few works by Severino Aznar, published at the beginning of the century,[1] the study of sociology in Spain was begun by Francisco Peiró with an essay on the reality of the socio-religious problem in Spain,[2] in which he tried to give a picture of the national situation; and by E. Vargas Zuñiga, who published a series of articles in *Razón y Fe* on "The Religious Problem in Spain".[3] We ought to include with these a study made by Arimón of the numbers of students in Spanish seminaries who persevere

---

* ROGELIO DUOCASTELLA: Born December 24, 1913 in Palau d'Anglesola, Spain, he was ordained in 1938 for the Diocese of Barcelona. He studied at the Diocesan Seminary of Barcelona, the University of Barcelona, Gregorian University in Rome and the Institut Catholique and the Sorbonne in Paris, earning his doctorate in social sciences. He is chaplain of the Asociación Católica Dirigentes de Sabadell, director of the Instituto de Sociología y Pastoral Aplicadas, and professor at the Seminario Hispanoamericano. He contributes frequently to the periodical *Social Compass*.

[1] S. Aznar, *El catolicismo social en España* (Madrid, 1906) and *Las grandes instituciones del catolicismo* (Madrid, 1912).

[2] F. Peiró, *El problema religioso-social en España* (Madrid, 1936).

[3] E. Vargas Zuñiga, "El Problema religioso en España," in *Razón y Fe*, 108, 109, 110 (1935-6).

in their vocation.[4] Just after the Civil War, Sarabia published a work that was intended to set people thinking about the real facts of the situation in Spain.[5] Yet we must say at once that these studies had nothing in common with modern scientific studies; they were hesitant stammerings rather than rigorously scientific studies. However, to do them credit, they did serve to open many eyes until then stubbornly closed to reality; and they did introduce Spain to the new science of sociology that had already progressed so much in other countries.

According to Professor le Bras, there were many reasons why Latin countries were slower than others in taking up the new science: "less documentation about local habits and customs, absence at that time of teams and competent organizations, persistence of unchanged pastoral methods." [6] In addition, we must include the following for Spain: the routine and traditional practice of religion that prevented people from realizing the existence of certain faults, or the superficiality into which many practices had fallen; the fact that religion had anchored itself to the traditional like a heavy rock; the lack of concern in the pastoral field —a sort of "resting on one's laurels". It was better for the peace of mind of many pastors not to worry too much. Spain was a Catholic country *with no problems*—a fatal mistake of which even now people are not sufficiently aware.

It seemed offensive to the simple piety of many Spaniards to think that Spanish Catholicism, monolithic as it was, could show the least flaw. It would have been a crime of disloyalty comparable to high treason.

For this reason the first studies moved cautiously and in general terms around certain aspects of Spanish religious life, without seeking to condemn the religious attitudes, which, in fact, were taken for granted. Because of this, time was spent preferably on such things as the manner in which the clergy were unevenly

---

[4] G. Arimón, *La enseñanza media en los seminarios de España* (Barcelona, 1935).

[5] R. Sarabia, *España es católica?* (Madrid, 1939).

[6] G. le Bras, "Présentation," in *Lumen Vitae* 6 (1951).

distributed in urban parishes, or the manner in which the people took part in divine worship, etc.

Since the Civil War there has been a greater uneasiness on the part of the younger generation, and many contacts have been established with other European countries. All this has awakened an interest in social studies, especially those that have been made in France. Several priests whom the Civil War had confronted with reality, engaged on their own account and at their own risk, in studies of this kind, generally as amateurs, but with admirable courage. Others, more fortunate, were able to visit the great European centers, especially in Paris and Belgium, to be trained in studies of this kind; but these efforts were usually of an individual nature, more from personal taste than with official diocesan sanction. Several priests and laymen of the diocese of Barcelona attended the first International Congress of Religious Sociology, and very soon made contact with LeBret's movement, "Economics and Humanism". Thanks to these isolated efforts the first steps were taken.

Soon after this the Jesuit Fathers in Madrid founded the review *Fomento Social,* which constantly focused people's attention on problems of religious sociology, though it would, perhaps, be more accurate to speak of "attitudes and religious mentality", as becomes apparent when we consider such articles as "A Glance at the Spanish Scene",[7] or, "What Is Causing the Breakup of Religion Among the Working Masses in Spain?"[8] Proper sociological studies, based on statistics, and worked out with scientific rigor, had not yet made their appearance.

In 1949 Severino Aznar, professor in the Central University, and considered one of the founders of sociology in Spain, published the first conscientious study of priestly vocations in Spain, and the effects on them of the years of the Republic and Civil War.[9] It was based on data solicited from all the Spanish semi-

[7] F. Del Valle, "Una Mirada al campo español," in *Fomento Social* 2 (1947).
[8] J. Azpiazu, "De donde nace la irreligiosidad de las masas trabajadoras en España?" in *Fomento Social* 4 (1949).
[9] S. Aznar, *La revolución española y las vocaciones eclesiásticas* (Madrid, 1949).

naries. A year later, M. Fraga Iribarne, in collaboration with J. Tena Artigas, conducted an inquiry among the university students at Madrid in order to find out a little about the "religious mentality" of Spanish youth.[10] As can be seen, we are still in the field of mere theory and essay.

Meanwhile, in the rest of Europe the reigning fashion was to see in religious sociology a valuable aid to pastoral work. By making use of a knowledge of the working area one could get better results (Boulard). In this it had already gone beyond the stage of collecting statistics, hardly entered as yet by Spain. After the delay referred to above, the first thing to enter Spain was a cult of numbers, of statistics, something much more within everyone's reach. It can be easily understood, therefore, that sociology should have been looked on with acute mistrust by traditionalists. Its importance was minimized, it was even treated with contempt. Some scoffed at "trying to regulate religion with numbers!"

In 1958 the first check on Sunday mass-attendance was made in the diocese of Santander.[11] Even though this diocese was considered to be rather conservative in matters of religious observance, the numbers revealed an unexpected state of affairs, and forced people to admit a real and hitherto unsuspected falling away. This was only a simple count of heads, without analysis or study of motives; but it was something!

Another indication that religious sociology was penetrating the field of theology was the fact that the theological reviews began to open their pages to studies in this subject, though it is generally true to say that they were of an empirical bent, *e.g.*, that of Leturia on "The Apostasy of the Masses".[12]

Finally, the efforts of an illustrious sociologist, Jesús Iribarren, one of the pioneers of the new science, materialized in the foundation of an Office of Information and Statistics of the Church, which was approved by the Spanish archbishops in 1950 and

[10] M. Fraga Iribarne and J. Tena Artigas, "Una encuesta a los universitarios de Madrid," in *Rev. Intr. Sociol.* 8 (1950).

[11] Francisco Odriozola Argos, *La asistencia a la misa en la diócesis de Santander* (Santander, 1959).

[12] P. Leturia, "La Apostasía de las masas," in *Rev. Esp. de Teología* 10 (1950).

opened in 1952. Since that time it has given much impetus to this sort of study, and has developed respectability, if not for religious sociology as a science, at least for the use of statistics in pastoral work, as, in fact, the very basis of such a study. The *Guia de la Iglesia en España,* published since 1954, amasses data and statistics on the religious life of Spain and has served as the basis of many later studies. Since that time, studies have proliferated, even if they revolve around problems of simple "stocktaking".

In 1951 the Most Rev. Enciso Viana, then Bishop of Ciudad Rodrigo, arranged an inquiry into attendance at mass in his diocese.[13] It was limited to a simple count of attendance by sex and status. Both facts show us clearly that what is catching on is an enthusiasm for statistics rather than religious sociology strictly speaking. (Nevertheless, statistics do have some value in that they force people to face up to reality, and abandon the complacent attitude of beatific contemplation in which Spanish Catholicism was fixed. The Church was recognizing that it had no right to boast of rosy clouds, and that it could not live forever on the heritage of the post-Reformation saints and mystics.) That year Archbishop Olaechea of Valencia also made an analysis of religious attitudes among the working classes,[14] and some years later founded the Instituto Social del Arzobispado.

In 1952 Bishop Morcillo of Bilbao ordered a study to be made of the extent to which the Sunday obligations were being observed in his diocese; this analysis followed the pattern set by previous inquiries.[15] Florentino Del Valle studied the economic and social problems of the city of Vigo,[16] and emphasized the problem of the de-christianization of the working class,[17] while

[13] J. Enciso Viana, "Resultados de la primera encuesta sobre asistencia a Misa," in *Bol. Obispado Ciudad Rodrigo* (1951).

[14] M. Olaechea, "Conclusiones de mi conocimiento del obrerismo valenciano," in *B.O.A.* VII (1951) and "Un sondeo en el alma del trabajador," in *Ecclesia* II (1951).

[15] C. Morcillo, "El precepto de la misa en la diócesis de Bilbao," in *B.O.A.* (1952).

[16] F. Del Valle, "Problemas económico-sociales de una ciudad moderna: Vigo," in *Razón y Fe* 142 (1951).

[17] *Idem,* "Hemos perdido la clase obrera en España?" in *Razón y Fe* 145 (1952).

Dr. Iribarren made progress in the field of family sociology.[18] During the two years following the first of these inquiries, Bishop Morcillo took up the problem of the observance of Easter duties, making the first investigation throughout the diocese of Bilbao.[19] Although we are once more in the field of statistics, still, it is a happy sign that the new fashion is catching on, at least in the more advanced and restless dioceses.

Nevertheless, the idea was spreading that it is very important to study the milieu when planning pastoral work. Now there is the National Secretariat for the Rural Apostolate (Secretariado Nacional de Apostolado Rural), which has undertaken the study of 81 towns in the area covered by the ancient kingdom of Leon-Castille, with explicitly pastoral ends in view.[20] This study, though it does not have the desired scientific rigor, is honest, and is very interesting in that the area studied was commonly held to be one of the more faithful in the matter of religious observances. The results of the study are very eloquent, and, like the previous ones, surprised quite a few people.

To Santos Beguiristiain belongs the distinction of having made the first study to combine religious sociology with pastoral theology, in which he recognizes and insists that sociological analysis is indispensable to pastoral work.[21]

A very important date in this history is 1955, the year in which Iribarren's *Introduccion a la Sociología Religiosa* appeared. In it he gives practical suggestions. It has been the source of many vocations, and has inspired many later studies. Iribarren comes midway between those who define sociology as "the science of society", and those who confuse it with theology. According to him, it is "the science of religious societies, of the social in religion".[22] It is, for him, a branch of general sociology, without amounting to a full-blown pastoral theology. One can detect in

---

[18] J. Iribarren, "Consideraciones estadísticas sobre la solidez de la familia española," in *Ecclesia* 3 (1953).

[19] C. Morcillo, *El cumplimiento pascual en la diócesis de Bilbao* (Bilbao, 1954).

[20] "Así son los pueblos. . . ." PYLSA (Madrid, 1954).

[21] S. Beguiristiain, *Una pastoral científica* (Bilbao, 1954).

[22] J. Iribarren, *Introduccion a la sociología religiosa* (Madrid, 1955).

him considerable influence from the *"Itineraires. . . ."* of Canon Boulard, which had been published in a Spanish translation the same year,[23] becoming the model for later studies. (This, by the way, explains why the majority of Spanish religious sociologists represents the tradition of France and Belgium, apart from the fact that many of them were trained there.)

In the same year there took place in Spain for the first time a *religious inquiry* in a large industrial city, *prepared in accordance with more modern scientific methods,* and in the tradition of authentic socio-religious investigation. The results of this extended study, in which were combined sociology, religious sociology, religious psychology and pastoral theology, were published piecemeal in various national and foreign publications, but they were not published as a whole until 1960.[24] Its author was the present writer, a disciple of le Bras and Boulard, and the study constituted his doctoral thesis at the Institut Catholique in Paris, 1957.

In 1956 I also carried into effect the first sociological and socio-religious analysis of the suburban areas of Barcelona, and at the same time proposed a way of carrying out pastoral work based on my findings.[25]

One by one, institutions have appeared whose work is confined to the field of religious sociology. Apart from those mentioned above, there have been created departments of the sociology of religion in the Higher Council for Scientific Investigations and in the Balmes Institute of Sociology. The latter, which was short-lived, was directed by M. Lizcano. In the Leo XIII Social Institute and in the Institute of Social Studies of Barcelona, chairs have been founded in this subject. The Dominicans have founded a sociographic center, Barrida y Vida, under the direction of J. M. Vázquez.

[23] F. Boulard, *Primeros pasos en sociología religiosa* (Vitoria, 1955).

[24] R. Duocastella, *Mataró: Estudio de sociología religiosa sobre una ciudad industrial española* (Barcelona, 1960).

[25] R. Duocastella, *Los suburbios de Barcelona* (Barcelona, 1957), also "El problema suburbial y sus consecuencias apostólicas," in *Ecclesia* (1957); "Disintegración urbana, fruto de las migraciones interiores," in *Ecclesia* 8/L (1958); "Se debe cortar la emigración?" in *Ecclesia* 8/L (1958).

It is interesting to note that in 1957 the present writer founded the first center of studies at a national level, under the auspices of Caritas Española (The Center for Studies in Applied Sociology), which gathered together for the first time all the experts in religious sociology. Its influence was the more notable since it was designed to cover the whole national ambit, and was intended to create a more favorable climate for the new science, and to dissipate anxieties about it.

In 1957 J. M. Mozaz published his *Teoría y tecnica de la encuesta religiosa,* in which he propounded methodological principles of undeniable interest.[26]

Little by little, religious sociology has approached the stage when it could be granted a certificate of naturalization, despite the fact that on the one hand it still meets with open opposition and undisguised mistrust, and on the other, it is beset by confusion among its very practitioners. There are no schools of thought. Everyone follows his own path, suggested by his own intuitions or personal circumstances. Nevertheless, every day brings more "seekers after the truth".

There has appeared a series of monograph studies that reveal at least a sincere unrest. Now the city of Cáceres has ordered an inquiry into Sunday mass-attendance;[27] J. M. de la Rica has analyzed the religious situation in a parish of Bilbao;[28] J. M. Vázquez has produced a study of a district of Madrid,[29] which he called a "sociographic study". J. A. Mateo confined himself to a suburban area of Madrid.[30] These followed, however, some studies of a more empirical turn,[31] some of which attack some

[26] J. M. Mozaz, *Teoría y técnica de la encuesta religiosa* (Vitoria, 1957).

[27] S. Rosado Dávila, "La asistencia a la Misa dominical en la ciudad de Cáceres" in *Ecclesia* 839 (1957).

[28] J. M. de la Rica, *La parroquia de Na.Sa. de las Mercedes de las Arenas. Estudio de Sociología Religiosa* (Bilbao, 1957).

[29] J. M. Vázquez, *Así viven y mueren* (Madrid, 1958).

[30] J. A. Mateo, "El Pozo del Tío Raimundo, reverso del gran Madrid," in *Razón y Fe* 149 (1959).

[31] Instituto Cultura Hispánica, *Catolicismo español, aspectos actuales* (Madrid, 1956); J. M. de Llanos, S.J., *Sentido individualista del catolicismo español;* M. Lizcano, "Etat et possibilités de la sociologie des re-

determined aspect such as demographic problems, particularly those relating to internal migrations[32] and priestly vocations.[33]

In 1958 Bishop Enciso Viana, who had been appointed to the diocese of Majorca, ordered a diocesan inquiry into the religious situation among his subjects, that would serve as a basis for a "pastoral drive".[34] It was the first time that a prelate had sought the aid of sociology to orient his pastoral work. (But we should, perhaps, more properly speak of "statistics" rather than "religious sociology".)

In 1959 I supervised the launching of an inquiry into Sunday mass-attendance in the whole of the diocese of Valencia, according to sex, age, social status, profession and parish. Sad to say, the final report, in spite of the wealth of data, was reduced to a mere tabulation of numbers![35] Presently it is the diocese of Segorbe, then that of Pamplona, etc.

Slowly, the Spanish hierarchy is beginning to take into account the importance of seeing religious sociology as the handmaid of pastoral work. The phrase of Pope Pius XII "to see clearly so as to be able to work more effectively", is being accepted. There are many prelates who ask for and encourage studies of religious sociology in order to become better acquainted with the truth of the situation that is hidden under the appearance of religion in their respective dioceses, so that they can orient their pastoral work. Among these we must single out the present Auxiliary Bishop of Ovideo, Most Rev. García de Sierra, who asked for a

---

ligions en Espagne," in *Arch. Soc. Rel.* 2 (1957); F. Del Valle, "Los avances de la sociología religiosa," in *Ecclesia* I (1957).

[32] C. Abaiuta, *Las migraciones interiores. Un nuevo capítulo en la pastoral contemporánea* (Seminario Vitoria, 1958); J. M. Diaz Mozaz, "Problemas que plantea la migración interior. Un quehacer político de urgencia," in *Ecclesia* 18/I (1958); R. Duocastella, "Problèmes d'adaptation dans le cas de migrations intérieures," in *Population* 1 (1957).

[33] J. M. Sans Vila, *Ciento tres vocaciones tardías* (Barcelona, 1955); R. Duocastella, *Problemas sacerdotales en España* (Madrid, 1959); J. Iribarren, "Podemos exportar vocaciones?" in *Ecclesia* 14 (1954); J. Guerrero, "Emigración de los religiosos a la ciudad," in *Razón y Fe* (1954).

[34] J. Enciso Viana, "Pastoral sobre el resultado de una encuesta diocesana," in *Bol. O. Mallorca* II (1958).

[35] Diócesis de Valencia, "Encuesta sobre la práctica religiosa," in B.O.A. (Nov. 1959).

study of the mining district of Langreo; the Bishop of Vitoria, who promoted the study of the whole city and diocese as a basis for orienting the work of the "Holy Mission" of 1962 (an important work was published almost immediately),[36] and more recently, the Bishop of Gerona, who has ordered a religio-sociological study of that part of his diocese next to the sea, and the effects on it of tourism. They are still working on it.

Aside from this preoccupation on the part of official pastors in their own spheres of interest, we find interesting projects undertaken in urban sociology.[37] We have also the most interesting study by Casiano Floristán,[38] presented as a doctoral thesis in the University of Tübingen, that constitutes an exhaustive analysis of worldwide trends in religious sociology and its points of contact with pastoral theology.

We must mention also the inquiry made by Miguel Benzo of the religious mentality of members of Madrid University;[39] the study of vocations made by Modesto Rexach[40] and J. M. Vázquez;[41] religious sociological studies of certain districts such as that made by Ivern, that made by D. J. Romeu of a suburban group in the city of Barcelona and that carried out by Vázquez in the Costa Brava,[42] commissioned by the Ministry of Tourism.

Apart from these studies, the activities that have developed on the fringe of religious sociology are legion: short courses and conferences in the Higher Institute of Religious Culture, in the Spanish-American seminary of O.C.S.H.A., in the Pontifical University of Salamanca, in the dioceses of Vitoria and Bilbao, in the theology faculty at Granada (Jesuit Fathers)—although not all with desirable regularity.

[36] R. Duocastella, J. Lorca and S. Misser, *Sociología y Pastoral de una diócesis: Vitoria* (Vitoria, 1964).

[37] J. Solá, "Sociología religiosa urbana," in *Razón y Fe* 161 (1960).

[38] C. Floristán, *Vertiente pastoral de la sociología religiosa* (Vitoria, 1960).

[39] M. Benzo, "Encuesta sobre la actitud religiosa en la facultad de ciencias de Madrid," in *Ecclesia*, col. 11, p. 809 (Feb. 1964).

[40] M. Rexach, *Las vocaciones sacerdotales en la diócesis de Vich* (Vich, 1959).

[41] J. M. Vázquez, *Las vocaciones en Galicia* (1958).

[42] *Idem*, Costa Brava. *Estudio de sociología religiosa* (Madrid, 1964).

In many parishes, especially in rural areas, and inspired by the National Secretariat for the Rural Apostolate, there have been some small-scale studies with popular appeal and several dissertations on religious sociological subjects. Many articles have been published in various reviews. But in spite of all this, we are still unable to talk of coordinated work, and much less of a "Spanish religious sociology". For the present, people are content that it should be a series of individual efforts, isolated, many of them important, nevertheless uncoordinated.

However, the recent step taken by the Spanish hierarchy in entrusting the present writer with the creation of an Institute of Sociology and Applied Pastoral Theology is extremely important. It is *ex professo* dedicated to such tasks and to the production of studies for the hierarchy, a work which, in fact, has been progressing now for many years. This Institute is nationally ambient, and is at the service of the Spanish Church, conducting inquiries and supplying data for social and pastoral work. It currently represents Spain at FERES (the International Federation of Social and Socio-Religious Research) in Belgium.

Finally, it is difficult to try to define clear and fundamental positions, to consider the nexus that exists between religious sociology and other ecclesiastical disciplines in Spain. In general, secular and some religious circles tend to regard religious sociology as such, as a theoretical science, as a "sociology of religion". Among priests, more responsible and conscious of their supernatural mission, the more knowledgeable take the position that sociology should be considered as a powerful aid to pastoral work.

Perhaps it will be several years before it is considered a truly ecclesiastical science, but we should not forget the words of Floristán: "To try to imagine pastoral activity with only the data of religious sociology would be an obvious distortion, since the basis of pastoral science is theological and is part of the data of revelation; but it would be rash to undertake pastoral work while turning a deaf ear to the data of the human situation, for Christianity is an historical as well as a supernatural religion."

Rosario Scarpati/*Sorrento, Italy*

Sociology and Pastoral Theology in Italy

In analyzing the state of pastoral sociology in Italy, it is well to bear in mind the dual role of sociology with respect to pastoral theology. On the one hand, it offers a "positive" contribution in concretizing pastoral "problems"; on the other, a "technical" contribution in assuring new avenues of approach and new methods of action. As far as Italy is concerned, the result is not too considerable; but there are certain areas of hope for the future.

I

SOCIOLOGICAL CONTRIBUTIONS TO PASTORAL THEOLOGY

As a positive discipline, sociology has up to now offered pastoral theology two distinct areas that often occur together: (1) sociographic studies, and (2) sociological research.

1. *Sociographic Studies*

In Italy, for one reason or another, sociology, after a promis-

---

* ROSARIO SCARPATI: Born May 22, 1930 in Sorrento, Italy, he was ordained in 1952 for the Diocese of Sorrento. He earned degrees in philosophy and theology. In his many published works he devotes himself especially to the problems of economic development and socio-religious integration. At present he is a professor of history and philosophy, consultor in sociology, and director of research for FERES.

ing beginning at the start of the century, underwent a veritable crisis. When it recovered, especially after World War II, it did not succeed in finding its true place. It was caught between the empirical methods (never very seriously pursued) of Anglo-Saxon origin and the rather theoretical tendencies of the German school. The observer found himself face to face with a series of investigations, fostered mostly by industry, the value of which was limited both by method and scope, while at the same time much writing was done on so-called "general problems". Indeed, some scholars continue analyzing the thought of the masters in excellent style, while others waste time on interdisciplinary areas without an adequate critical preoccupation with the problems of integration facing us at every turn.

This general tendency has been felt in the area of religious sociology. There are, indeed, many studies on religious practice on the parish level, and even for the diocese, but these rarely attain a scientific level. Efforts that would give substance to a group of specialists and some measure of guarantee that their selection of hypotheses would be valid, their methodology clear and adapted to their environment, and some technique of comparative analysis that could concretize their first empirical generalizations, have failed. Hence, we had in the area of religious sociology a series of fragmentary and regional studies that could offer no sufficient basis for comparison. Consequently, they were ineffectual at the very point of attacking true problems and relevant solutions. Up to now, this lack of orientation has made it impossible to produce a serious outline of some kind of religious map of Italy, the usefulness of which is clear to all. The only guarantees of scientific precision come from those centers and institutes that have good internal organization, and, through the support of the hierarchy, an articulated program and a continuous plan of work. Such, for example, is the center of socio-religious research at Bologna.

2. Sociological Research

Consequently, even sociological investigations have not succeeded in attaining any importance or the value that they merit. For them, on the other hand, even more than the aforementioned studies, there is need of a bit of the "sociological spirit", that is, an intellectual approach together with more definite organization of the work at hand. In Italy this is only beginning. It is supported by the fact that investigations of a very high caliber, such as those by P. G. Grasso on transitional values in the adolescent world, remain isolated from the general context and cannot express all the dialectical richness they really possess.

Next, the tendency to studies of a "general nature", though they produce facile conclusions at the diagnostic stage, has never succeeded in provoking a type of scientific rapport that would allow coordinated study, as for example of the religious mentality of a group or a particular area. In addition, this lack of cooperation and of information prevented the full utilization of the results, which, as we know, could be enriched by critical discussion.

It is easy to conclude that religious sociology has not been able to contribute sufficiently to the concretization of the problems of pastoral theology in Italy, even though some statistics and some essays have raised disturbing questions among pastors.

II

The Renewal of Pastoral Theology

The renewal of pastoral theology must embrace not only problems of a theological nature, such as those discussed at Vatican Council II, but also many problems of a frankly sociological nature. The analysis and solution of these are intimately connected, precisely because pastoral theology is nothing else than a prolongation of the mystery of the incarnation. If the sociology of religion, as we have seen, has given only a negligible contribution to the solution of pastoral problems, it has not yet succeeded in finding a way of developing structures and techniques for a pastoral theology adapted to the times. And this for two reasons:

(1) the absence of live debate or any theologico-pastoral reflection upon positive data, and (2) the lack of any institutional structures in which analyses and concrete solutions in practice could be permanently stored. In the first instance, there is an intellectual deficiency and the absence of a scientific point of view; in the second, the lack of a practical spirit and a too superficial definition of tasks, competence and responsibility. This situation, too, might easily be reduced to more or less historical causes, falling in the general area of the religious underdevelopment of Italy. But the reality is so complex that to describe it so superficially hardly suggests a serious scientific approach. Let us try, nonetheless, to sketch a more immediate explanation.

1. *Theologico-Pastoral Reflections*

Insofar as a concrete and modern pastoral theology is concerned, we can well admit that the situation has improved over the last few years. The insufficient level of important studies (which alone can raise questions with theologians), and an ambiguous interpretation of the role of religious sociology has slowed down progress considerably. It must be admitted that the tradition of Italian theology has always had a metaphysical bent, and only after the war has it taken a positive direction. Doubtless, the method of study and, more specifically, the historical approach in the treatment of theological problems is the true avenue toward cooperation in putting to use all the pastoral wealth of the traditional scholastic teaching, and also to develop a sense of dialogue with the other disciplines. Theology has too long been confined to areas that are exclusively ecclesiastical; indeed, its teachers have too easily identified the superiority of its formal object with the exclusion of any other branch of knowledge of a practical sort.

On the other hand, the socio-religious approach, admittedly begun under good auspices on the statistical level in 19th-century Italy, has not found a good circle of specialists who could inaugurate a dialogue in correct and energetic terms with theologians and especially with teachers of pastoral theology. The work of Leone in the diocese of Mantua in 1954 was sufficient to provoke a series of problems and questions that surely assisted in the birth and the development of centers and the work of individual specialists actually working in Italy, while these, too, occasioned the first writings of theologians on the vital problems of pastoral theology. Today, this work is still only beginning. But there are some consoling signs: the work envisaged at the Center in Bologna, the presence of specialists in the first centers or commissions with a pastoral orientation, and conferences such as the one organized at Taranto in April 1964 on the significant theme, "Industrialization and Pastoral Theology".

2. *Institutional Structures*

With regard to institutional structures, which in practice are the "pastoral commissions", "secretariats" or "departments" under the guidance of the episcopate, the situation is somewhat more fluid in Italy than elsewhere. The most difficult point, as experts have noted, is the definition of the real power of the episcopal conferences insofar as they are a practical extension of the episcopal college. The uncertainty that surrounds this point is reflected in the entire juridical structure and in all the operational procedures of modern pastoral theology. Where the habit of discussion, the decentralization of power, and more often, the urgency of the immediate problems have given rise to certain emergency procedures and channels of information and collaboration, the problem today remains one of adaptation or revision of what already exists, on the basis of experience.

In Italy we have the advantage of starting from the very beginning. Elsewhere, the problems that the episcopal conference should face have been so clearly presented by Pope Paul VI that no further comment is necessary. At any rate, such problems may demand a practical mind, a clear division of the tasks to be performed and a lively sense of responsibility; and this in practice means embracing as a preliminary and (later) integral part the entire contribution made by the sociology of religion. Indeed, sociology can and must rise to the actual elaboration of pastoral procedures and to the projection of actual techniques of action and communication. Vatican Council II, in proposing the *aggiornamento* of the Church, has indeed already indicated the principles of the solution, so that pastoral sociology might become one of the indispensable disciplines of the Church to respond to the signs of the times and put into practice the conciliar decrees.

Let us conclude by saying that pastoral sociology, so far as Italy is concerned, does not yet present a positive picture, but it does hold up hope that allows us to predict a slow but certain evolution.

BIBLIOGRAPHY

Acquaviva, S. S. "Un primo contributo alla sociologia storico-religiosa del Padovano," in *Sociologia religiosa* 3-4 (1960), pp. 86-7.
——— *L'eclisse del sacro nella società industriale.* Milan: Communita, 1961.
Burgalassi, S. "La sociologia religiosa in Italia dal 1955," in *Vita sociale* 17 (1960), pp. 35-47.
——— "Sintesi religiosa dell'Italia," in *Il Regno* 5 (1960), pp. 20-4.
Leoni, A. *Sociologia e geografia religiosa di una Diocesi.* Roma: Gregoriana, 1953.
——— *Aggiornamento e processo di adeguamento degli istituti religiosi femminili alle osigenze della società italiana.* Roma: Supplemento ALA, 1953.
Scarpati, R. "La ricerca socio-religiosa come sussidio pastorale," in *Orientamenti Pastorali* 3 (1964), pp. 75-84.

GENERAL BIBLIOGRAPHY

GENERAL STUDIES

Boulard, F. *Premiers Itinéraires en Sociologie Religieuse*. Paris: Ed. Ouvrières, 1954.

Carrier, H. *Psycho-sociologie de l'appartenance religieuse*. Rome: Gregoriana, 1964.

Dingemans, L., Houtart, F. *Pastorale d'une Région industrielle*. Brussels: CEP, 1964.

Fichter, J. H. *Social relations in the Urban Parish*. University of Chicago, 1954.

Goddijn, W., Goddijn, H. P. *Godsdienstsociologie*. Utrecht: Spectrum, 1960.

Houtart, F. *Sociologie et Pastorale*. Paris: Fleurus, 1963.

———— *L'Eglise latino-américaine à l'heure du Concile* (English and Spanish translations). Fribourg: FERES, 1962.

Izarny, R. *L'Eglise et la Ville*. Paris: Desclée, 1958.

Labbens, J. *L'Eglise et les Centres urbains*. Paris: Spes, 1959.

Laloux, J. *Problèmes actuels du monde rural*. Brussels: La Pensée catholique, 1957.

———— *Mettre l'Eglise en Etat de Mission*. Brussels: CEP, 1964.

Luzbetak, L. *The Church and Cultures: An Applied Missionary Anthropology*. Techny, Illinois: Divine Word Publications, 1963.

Le Bras, G. "Réflexions sur les différences entre Sociologie scientifique et Sociologie pastorale," in *Archives de la Sociologie des Religions* 8 (1959), pp. 5-14.

Neundorfer, L. "Methoden der Pastoralsoziologie," in *Anima* 12 (1957).

Pin, E. *Elementos para una sociologia del Catolicismo latino-americano*. Bogota: FERES, 1963.

———— "Sociologie ou pastorale?" in *Revue de l'Action Populaire* 128 (1959), pp. 589-95.

Schurr, V. *Die Pastoralsoziologie* (Seelsorge in Einer Neuen Welt, 1957), pp. 109-35.

Virton, P. *Enquêtes de sociologie paroissiale*. Paris: Spes, 1953.

Zeegers, G. H. "De 'social research' als apostolisch Instrument," in *Social Compass* 3 (1955), pp. 81-4.

Tufari, P. "Ricerca e intervento di sociologia della religione," in *Rassegna italiana di sociologia* 1 (1960), pp. 102-21.

———— *Pastorale d'aujourd'hui*. (Italian translation). Brussels: CEP, 1962.

———— *Paroisses urbaines et paroisses rurales*. Tournai: Casterman, 1958.

———— *Vocation de la Sociologie et Sociologie des Vocations*. Tournai: Casterman, 1958.

AFRICA

Chelodi, J. *Introduction à la sociologie de l'Islam*. Paris: Maisonneuve, 1958.

Houtart, F. "Aspects sociologiques de l'Eglise au Congo," in *Afrikakring* 7 (1960), pp. 45-55.

Noirhomme, J. *L'Eglise au Congo*. Léopoldville: Centre de recherches socio-religieuses, 1963.

Parsons, R. T. "Missionary-African Relations," in *Civilisations* 4 (1953), pp. 505-18.

Pratt, J. A. "Spiritual Conflicts in a Changing Africa," in *The Ecumenical Review* 8 (1956), pp. 154-62.

Ross, E. "Impact of Christianity on Africa," in *Annals* 298, pp. 161-9.

LATIN AMERICA

Apart from the socio-religious study of this continent undertaken by FERES in 1958 under the direction of F. Houtart and published in three collections containing some forty articles, we mention the following:

Alonso, I. *La Iglesia en América, Estructuras eclesiasticas*. Bogota: FERES, 1964.

Alonso, I., Garrido, G. *La Iglesia en América Central y el Caribe, Estructuras eclesiasticas*. Bogota: FERES, 1963.

Alonso, I., Garrido, G., Dammert, M., Bellido, Tumiri, J. *La Iglesia en Peru y Bolivia, Estructuras eclesiasticas*. Bogota: FERES, 1961.

Alonso, I., Luzardo, M., Garrido, G., Oriol, J. *La Iglesia en Venezuela y Ecuador, Estructuras eclesiasticas*. Bogota: FERES, 1961.

Amato, E. *La Iglesia en Argentina*. Bogota: FERES, 1961.

Alonso, I., Acha, A., Garmendia, J. de. *La Iglesia en Paraguay y Uruguay*. Bogota: FERES, 1963.

Damboriena, P. *El Protestantismo en América Latina*. Bogota: FERES, 1963.

Estepa, J. M., Diaz, J. *La Liturgia y la catequesis en América Latina*. Bogota: FERES, 1964.

Perez, G. *El problema sacerdotal en América Latina*. Bogota: FERES, 1961.

Perez, G., Wust, I. *La Iglesia en Colombia*. Bogota: FERES, 1962.

Poblete, R. *La Iglesia en Chile*. Bogota: FERES, 1961.

Ramos, R., Alonso, I. *La Iglesia en Mexico*. Bogota: FERES, 1964.

Bastide, R. *Les religions afro-brésiliennes*. Paris, 1960.

Gonzales Pineda, F. *El Mexicano: su dinamismo psico-social*. Mexico: Pax, 1959.

Houtart, F. "Les conditions sociales de la pastorale dans les grandes villes de l'Amérique latine," in *Social Compass* 5 (1958), pp. 181-99.

NORTH AMERICA

Abbott, M. M. *A City Parish Grows and Changes*. Washington: Catholic University, 1954.

Allport, G. W., Gillespie, J. P., Young, J. "The Religion of Post-War College Students," in *Journal of Psychology* 25 (1948), pp. 3-33.

Bor Broen, W. E. "A Factor Analytic Study of Religion," in *Journal of Abnormal and Social Psychology* 54 (1957), pp. 176-9.

Carrier, H. "La religion des étudiants américains: synthèse des recherches," in *Archives de la Sociologie des Religions* 12 (1961), pp. 89-102.

Early, I. D. "The Sociology of Religion in the United States," in *Sociologia religiosa* 7 (1961), pp. 85-100.

Fichter, J. H. *Southern Parish I: Dynamics of a City Church*. University of Chicago, 1961.

———— *Social Relations in an Urban Parish*. University of Chicago, 1954.

———— *Parochial School*. University of Notre Dame, 1958.

———— *Religion as an Occupation*. University of Notre Dame, 1961.

Glock, C. Y., Ringer, B. B. "Church Policy and the Attitude of Ministers and Parishioners on Social Issues," in *American Sociological Review* 21 (1958), pp. 148-56.

Greeley, A. M. *The Church and the Suburbs*. New York: Sheed & Ward, 1961.

Herberg, W. *Protestant-Catholic-Jew*. New York: Doubleday, 1961. (French translation, Paris: Spes, 1962).

Houtart, F. *Aspects sociologiques du Catholicisme Américain*. Paris: Economie et Humanisme, 1957.

Lacoste, N. *Les caractéristiques sociales de la population du Grand Montréal*. University of Montreal, 1958.

Lambert, R. D. (ed.) "Religion in American Society," in *Annals*, 332, 1961.

Madden, L. A. *Role-Definitions of Catholic Sister Educators and Expectations of Students, Their Parents and Teaching Sisters*. Washington: Catholic University, 1960.

Moberg, D. O. *The Church as a Social Institution*. Englewood Cliffs, New Jersey: Prentice Hall, 1962.

Nimkoff, M. L., Wood, A. L. "Effect of Majority Patterns on the Religious Behavior of Minority Group," in *Sociological and Social Research* 30 (1946), pp. 282-9.

Nuesse, G., Harte, T. J. *The Sociology of the Parish*. Milwaukee, Wisconsin: Bruce, 1951.

O'Dea, T. F. *The American Catholic Dilemma*. New York: Sheed & Ward, 1958.

Page, J. E. *Catholic Parish Ecology and Urban Development in the Greater Winnipeg*. Winnipeg, 1958.

Parsons, T. "The Cultural Background of American Religious Organizations," in *Proceedings of the Conference on Science, Philosophy and Religion*, 1960.

———— "The Patterns of Religious Organization in the United States," in *Daedalus* (1958), pp. 65-85.

Schuyler, J. B. *Northern Parish: a Sociological and Pastoral Study*. Chicago: Loyola University, 1960.

Schnepp, G. J. *Leakage from a Catholic Parish*. Washington: Catholic University, 1942.

EUROPE

FRANCE

Babin, P. *Les Jeunes et la Foi*. Lyons: Chatelet, 1961.

Boulard, F. "Carte religieuse de la France rurale," in *Cahiers du Clergé rural* 92 (1947), pp. 403-14.

———— *Problèmes missionaires de la France rurale*. Paris: Ed. du Cerf, 1945.

———— *Essor ou Déclin du Clergé français?* Paris: Ed. du Cerf, 1950.

Chelini, J. *Genèse et évolution d'une paroisse suburbaine marseillaise*. Marseille: Saint Léon, 1953.

Daniel, Y. *Aspects de la pratique religieuse à Paris.* Paris: Ed. Ouvrières, 1952.

Isambert, F. A. *Christianisme et classes ouvrières.* Tournai: Casterman, 1953.

Klaine, R. "Metz: la ville et l'Eglise," in Metz: supplément à la *Revue Ecclésiastique,* 1959.

Labbens, J. *Les 99 autres.* Lyons: Vitte, 1954.

—— *La pratique dominicale dans l'agglomération lyonnaise.* (3 Vol.) Lyons, 1955.

Le Bras, G. *Introduction à l'histoire de la pratique religieuse en France.* (2 Vol.) Paris: Presses Universitaires, 1942-45.

—— *Etudes de sociologie religieuse.* Paris: Presses Universitaires, 1955.

—— *La pratique religieuse dans les villes et dans les campagnes.* Paris: Colin, 1950.

Luchini, A. M. *L'agglomération dijonaise.* Dijon: Sec. de la Mission, 1959.

Maitre, J. "Les dénombrements des catholiques pratiquants," in *Archives de la Sociologie des Religions* 5 (1960), pp. 72-95.

Pin, E. *Pratique religieuse et classes sociales dans une paroisse urbaine.* Paris: Spes, 1956.

Poulat, E. "La découverte de la ville par le catholicisme français contemporain," in *Annales* 15 (1960), pp. 1168-79.

Pourchet, G. "Aperçu sociologique sur le monde ouvrier," in *Masses ouvrières* 129 (1957), pp. 35-80.

Schmitt-Eglin, P. *Le mécanisme de la déchristianisation: recherche pastorale sur le peuple des campagnes.* Paris: Alsatia, 1952.

Verscheure, J., Deprost, S., Traulle, C. *Aspects sociologiques de la pratique religieuse dominicale* (Diocèse de Lille). Lille: CDESR, 1961.

THE NETHERLANDS

Mention must first be made of the work published by the Katholiek Sociaal Kerkelijk Instituut (K.S.K.I.), founded by Prof. G. Zeegers in 1946, and extending over many fields of research.

Arntz, A. J. "Les catholiques hollandais dans la nation," in *Vie intellectuelle* 2 (1955), pp. 137-52.

Dellepoort, J. *De Priesterroepingen in Nederland.* The Hague, 1955.

Goddijn, W. "The Sociology of Religion and Socio-Religious Research in the Netherlands," in *Social Compass* 7 (1960), pp. 361-9.

Godefroy, J. "De toekomstige Behoefte aan Docenten bij het Katholiek Onderwijs in Nederland," in *Social Compass* 2 (1954), pp. 168-82.

Matthijssen, M. A. *Katholiek Middelbaar Onderwijs en intellectuele Emancipatie.* Assen, 1958.

Van Leeuwen, B. *Het Gemengde Huwelijk.* Assen, 1959.

Zeegers, G. "Sociology of Religion in the Netherlands," in *American Catholic Sociological Review* 5 (1954), pp. 176-89.

GREAT BRITAIN

Brothers, J. *Church and School.* University of Liverpool, 1964.

Spencer, A. E. "Catholic Marriages," in *Tablet,* March 14, 1959.

—— "The Irish Catholics in England," in *Tablet,* July 22, 1959.

Ward, C. K. *Priests and People.* University of Liverpool, 1961.

Victor Schurr/*Munich, W. Germany*

Kerygma and Dogma

In this article the words "kerygma" and "dogma" are both used in the wider sense. "Kerygma" does not refer here merely to the first proclamation of the events of salvation (missionary preaching), but it includes every proclamation of God's Word. Above all, it includes the Word of God as officially proclaimed by the Church in praise of God and for the salvation of man. "Kerygma", then, is the call addressed by God in Christ to man requiring a response. "Dogma" does not merely refer here to official definitions of faith and morals. It includes all Christian truth presented as something to be learned and consented to. In other words, dogma speaks *about* God, in kerygma God himself speaks (cf. Heb. 12, 25). This article deals with the relation between dogma and kerygma from the theologico-pastoral point of view in order to assist the Church in her saving mission.

I

History of the Problem

If we look at the problem as one of "acceptance of revelation in view of personal salvation" and of our "attitude toward revela-

---

* Victor Schurr, C.SS.R.: Born April 4, 1898 in Düsseldorf, Germany, he became a Redemptorist and was ordained in 1925. He studied at Gregorian University, Rome, earning his doctorate in theology in 1935. His experience is broad: lector of dogmatic theology at the Redemptorist Seminary in Munich, professor of pastoral theology at the Academia Alfonsiana in Rome, director of the Pastoral Institute at Munich, editor-in-chief of the periodical *Theologie der Gegenwart,* co-editor of the periodical *Lebendige Seelsorge* and consultor for homiletics in *Lexikon für Theologie und Kirche.*

tion", then it is as old as the history of revelation. It began to dominate contemporary theology during the last decades when Christian reality seemed to evaporate in a changing society; when, under the influence of Kierkegaard and Heidegger, truth shifted toward concrete expression and linguistic facts; when there was less appreciation of the objective elements and the distinction between object and subject was abandoned.

After the school of "liberal" theology had failed in its attempt to provide an authentic account of the life of Jesus on the basis of history and philology, scholars tried to find a genuine theological approach to the New Testament. The key word became "kerygma": "The real (*i.e.,* actual and effective) Christ is Christ as he was preached" (M. Kähler); the traditional elements of the New Testament owe their origin to the kerygma (M. Dibelius). The real development of this view was the work of R. Bultmann: historical incidents, concrete facts connected with salvation are of no interest to the faithful; Jesus did not rise from the tomb but from the kerygma, *i.e.,* his presence is actual in the preaching. Faith is a paradoxical gamble; through the New Testament itself man comes to understand it and his own existence (existential interpretation). The core of this self-understanding, buried in the "mythological" account of the New Testament, must be laid bare for modern man and lead him to make his decisive choice (not to knowledge).

Bultmann's disciples, G. Bornkamm, E. Fuchs, G. Ebeling and others, are today turning away from this view. They ask: What really lies behind this preaching? They stress again the importance of the historical Jesus, not in order to strengthen the faith, but in order to show forth Jesus as witness, exemplar and helper, as the "author and finisher of faith" (Heb. 12, 2). With all this there persists among Protestants the same attitude as before, which opposes subjective faith to the objective contents of the faith, an attitude that developed with Adolph von Harnack (Christianity is undogmatic) and continued until John A. T. Robinson who discards all metaphysics and maintains that only existential knowledge is legitimately possible.

Among Catholics the relation between kerygma and dogma never became the subject of such heated controversy. Yet, the problem was there, for instance in the debate about the new approach to catechetics: should the method used be based on the new scholastic treatment of dogma or on psychology (the Munich school)? These latter methods proceeded in four stages: introduction, presentation, explanation and application, the same manner in which a subject is presented in secular teaching.

Recently G. Weber suggested a method that is more personal and better adjusted to the process of salvation and pastoral care. He proceeds in three stages: preaching, reflection and realization. Our problem is still more directly implied in the controversy about the theology of preaching of the Innsbruck school. This school demands, apart from scientific ("scholastic") theology with its formal object, "the true" (God, under the aspect of Deity—*Deus sub ratione deitatis*), another theology for the pastoral training of the clergy with its formal object "the good" as the subject of preaching (*bonum praedicabile* = Christ).

The "Nouvelle Théologie" of France (1940-1950) aimed at reviving theology through the Bible, patristics and contemporary philosophy, and envisaged both the immutability and the historic character of the truth. Important progress was made in the theology of Karl Rahner and his school (J. B. Metz and others) with its demand for existential concepts more in tune with revelation; this brings dogma and preaching of the Word together in a way that makes a separate theology for pastoral care unnecessary.

Lastly, I must mention the conflict between conservative and progressive views at Vatican Council II. Time and again schemata were sent back because they were too scholastic, not biblical enough and too little in touch with our fellow Christians and the world. The whole Council is involved in a cathartic process that leads from an archaic theology preoccupied with essences to a kerygmatic and pastoral theology for today. This diminishes or eliminates the constant tension between intellectual objects and personal reality.

II

DISCUSSION

Since the kerygma, the proclamation, of the Word of God takes place in human words, it is preceded by thought rooted in being and tending to express itself in objective concepts. But in the proclamation itself this element is practically left out. It is not primarily a matter of communicating religious doctrine, nor of providing information about historical events concerned with salvation. Kerygma is an "address", a "speaking to", in which "at that moment the event of Jesus Christ becomes present, and present as an event which affects me in my own existence" (Bultmann).

Christ's first disciples saw their existence revolutionized through the resurrection of the Lord, and from then on they could not do otherwise than proclaim and bear witness to the events connected with Jesus as the "evangel", the Good News (Acts 4, 20). And this was not because of the message in itself, but so that "everyone may turn from his wickedness" (Acts 3, 26). This proclamation inaugurated the reign of the glorified *Kyrios,* the Lord in glory. The mere fact that the action of God's love became perceptible, and thus present, in Christ (compare, *e.g.,* Col. 1, 18 with 1 Cor. 11, 26), it expressed praise and worship of God; that is why the kerygma reaches its climax in the celebration of the eucharist (1 Cor. 11, 26). As it developed, this kerygma did not lead in the first place to objective reflection but to the application of what was transmitted to the present situation and its concerns (see, *e.g.,* the parable of the weeds, Matt. 13, 24-43). This was not a strange procedure for the transmission of the truth. The kerygma or proclamation is never mere history—the exact narration of some past happening—but is something existential and eschatological. The Holy Spirit, whose role it is to make present and to change, brings the truth into the subjective situation where it is assimilated in a personal manner. Thus he makes the truth more true than if it were a purely objective communication. What *happened* in the kerygma was the main thing, and from there its contents took shape in word and writing; this led to teaching, dogma and rules of faith, a process that can only become salutary when first the ground is prepared for conversion by personal encounter, by event and witness. The truth is therefore truly a person, Christ.

The original kerygma of the Church provides the contents and the exemplar for our preaching. It is the exemplar because it is definitive in essence. One may reason this out in the following way:

In the proclamation or announcement the active revelation of the Word becomes, through the grace working in the recipient, a subjective principle in the preacher, the hearer and in the Church at large. This makes faith possible, which is the free acceptance of God's Word. In this first phase in which God first communicates himself, the faith is transcendental and not yet specified; it is, so to speak, the horizon and light of all that follows. In the kerygma it must therefore penetrate before everything else, create the ambiance for decisive attitudes and the medium for standards that are totally different from those of the "world". "I believed, and so I spoke" (2 Cor. 4, 13). God's Word and faith belong essentially together.

In the second phase the Word of God penetrates into the region of concepts and categories, and expresses itself in corresponding statements. These statements are not purely material, static or historical, but rather personal, living, eventful. This is not because Scripture took over the Semitic use of words that was close to the surrounding concrete world (the word used as something dynamic, as opposed to the Greek use which is mainly noetic), but because in the kerygma God draws near in living events, urges on toward self-fulfillment and this is beyond a purely material relationship. This existential character of the kerygma marks all that is contained in God's Word, and gives it its dramatic quality. It turns the "everlasting gospel" (Apoc. 14, 6) into a saving event, constantly present and fitted into every situation.

This does not mean that the Church is only built up through the power (*dynamis*) of the Word (1 Cor. 2, 1-4). The Church also needs human intelligence (*dianoia*) at all times. The rational element (which should never be taken in isolation) has its place, first of all, in the human approaches to the faith. Without going back to the historical events, the kerygma and Christ after the first Easter would appear to human reason (if not perverted) as unrealistic docetic talk, and faith could not present itself as intellectually and morally necessary (the task of fundamental theology, and the justification of apologetics, that secondary kind of preaching). Faith is not divine because rational preliminary assurances have been destroyed or ignored. There is no need to fear that the personal element will make of God something purely objective, or something secular or a matter of indifference. The idea of "God as some cosmic phenomenon like everything else" is explicitly rejected by theological thought, while analogy leads from what is an objective statement to the infinite personality of God. Moreover, as has already been pointed out, the factual truth of the faith is not presented in its basic essence but rationally: "God has truly spoken". Yet, it should be remembered that a leap in the dark can only lead to Christ instead of Socrates, when one lives already *de facto* in a Christian environment. It is wrong to pretend one cannot reach a completely different understanding of oneself except through the Bible. In an alien or distant cultural epoch it is possible to take as norm of the truth an unselfish surrender to God that is not prompted by knowledge of the cross, since the Bible would have no appeal for the then prevalent experience. Moreover, we have reached today a more positive evaluation of non-Christian religions and we admit that pagans can attain salvation even when the outward revelation of the Word in the Bible has not reached them (anonymous Christians). We hold then that the preaching and faith which were given us in a human manner, must be taken in their totality, and therefore have acceptable rational and objective foundations.

Secondly, the dramatic character of the kerygma contains *in itself* a store of dogmatic content which, through reflection, explanation and synthesis, is conceptually expressed in doctrine and system (*fides quaerens intellectum*). This process can already be observed in the original kerygma of Scripture. Particularly in the pastoral letters one can already see the transition from the kerygma to an established doctrine which became the norm in the Church's teaching. Through the Church's magisterium the dogma becomes the *proxima regula fidei,* and watches over the growth of this preaching by clarifying, confirming and guiding it in truth and intelligibility. It has therefore great significance for pastoral work.

To this must be added that, wherever God's message is received in a living manner, it is linked with the life of the preacher, the hearer, the contemporary society, and this means that the message as conveyed is not purely kerygmatic but mixed with dogmatic or theological elements. Because of the historical condition of man there is no such thing as a *sola scriptura* or *solum kerygma:* it is always mixed with other realities, experience, philosophy, etc. Thus, the proclamation unfolds, becomes specific and dogmatic. This is not an evil, because through this preaching the once given revelation is constantly adapted to place and time. It is brought into a new reality and a new situation, and this necessarily gives it a dogmatic form. Dogma, therefore, enlarges the contents of the kerygma by adding existential, speculative (cf. Denzinger, 1529) and secular elements to it (this is now also admitted by K. Barth, *Die kirchliche Dogmatik* IV, 3). All things, then, have received their being from the Logos and inwardly tend toward Christ as their end.

It must also be noted that preaching takes place with the visible community or the Church in view (1 John 1, 3) and so aims at *communal* faith, understanding, witness and consequently at explicit specification: its action can only be lasting in what is communal and all-embracing.

The Mover of the whole (kerygma and dogma) is the Spirit that blows where it wills. God has made himself present to us not only in the Son but also in the Spirit. Where God creates, he creates a cosmos, a world. The rational structure of preaching and teaching must not be despised, and dogma not be rejected.

On the other hand, this teaching must not become an isolated and aimless enterprise. The essential basis of all dogmatic and theological thinking is the faith. Without it the theologian is but a student of religion. Because of this, theology is related to revelation and salvation history. Born of the events of salvation and of faith, it is involved in the realization of this salvation and the extension of the kerygma, although it is immediately concerned with knowledge. The preaching is not there for the doctrine but the doctrine is there for the preaching. The Church's magisterium (as *norma a Scriptura normata*) and dogma abide under the primacy and in the framework of the kerygma. Considered as a whole, the Christian reality knows no legitimate "in se", no self-contained and self-centered part; everything tends toward the "pro nobis" (John 3, 15) with all its implications, and it must not be pushed in the direction of one-sided, essential, rationally satisfying and specific teaching.

Existential meaning demands objectivity, and preaching demands dogma, and both are dominated by the kerygma. This interrelationship is healthy and makes each fruitful (Denzinger, 1796). Nevertheless there remains tension: dogma can never adequately contain the kerygma, the Word of God; and even dogma itself can never express the fullness and mystery of all that it contains. Particularly, neither preaching nor dogma can be fully translated into life although both aim at this either directly or indirectly.

From what has been said we may conclude that the primacy belongs to the kerygma. Pastoral care, dogma and theology must above all be penetrated by *its* original statements, the faith and its existential categories. This makes it the more imperative that dogma should test the Church's preaching, so that it does not wander off into the clouds, but reaches the full scope of contemporary life in a way that is to the point, compelling and total. In doing this, dogma fulfills itself in pastoral care. In brief: "Dogmatic theology is the conscience of the preacher, and preaching is the conscience of the dogmatic theologian" (H. Ott).

BIBLIOGRAPHY

Barth, K. *Church Dogmatics: Doctrine of Reconciliation.* Scribners, 1957.
Bartsch, H. W. *Kerygma und Mythos.* Hamburg-Bergstedt, I 1948, II 1952, III 1954, IV 1955, V 1955, VI 1963.
Bohren, R. *Predigt und Gemeinde.* Zürich-Stuttgart, 1963.
Bultmann, R. *Glauben und Verstehen.* Tübingen, I 1933, II 1952, III 1960.
Ebeling, G. *Ein Gespräch mit R. Bultmann.* Tübingen, 1962.
Fuchs, E. "Zur Frage nach dem historischen Jesus," in *Gesammelte Aufsätze* II (Tübingen, 1960).
Gollwitzer, H. *Die Existenz Gottes im Bekenntnis des Glaubens.* Munich, 1963.
Hunter, A. M. *Teaching and Preaching in the New Testament.* London, 1963.
Jentsch, W. "Verkünden und Verstehen," in *Handbuch der Jugendseelsorge,* part II, "Theologie der Jugendseelsorge" (Gütersloh, 1963), pp. 204-53.
Jungmann, J. A. *Handing on the Faith.* Herder and Herder, 1959.
Kählin, M. *Der sog. historische Jesus und der geschichtliche, biblische Christus.* Leipzig, 1892; new ed. by E. Wolf, Munich, 1953, ²1956.
Metz, J. B. *Christliche Anthropozentrik. Über die Denkform des Thomas von Aquin.* Munich, 1962.
Moore, S. "The Word of God: Kerygma and Theorem," in *The Heythrop Journal* 5 (1964), pp. 268-75.
Ott, H. *Dogmatik und Verkündigung.* Berlin, 1961.
Pannenberg, W. and Rahner, K. "Zum Problem der dogmatischen Aussage," in E. Schlink and H. Volk (ed.), *Pro Veritate* (Münster and Kassel, 1963), pp. 239-385.
Ratzinger, J. "Christozentrik in der Verkündigung," in *Trierer theologische Zeitschrift* 70 (1961), pp. 7-14.
Ristow, H. and Matthiae, K. (ed.). *Der historische Jesus und der kerygmatische Christus,* 1960.
Robinson, John A. T. *Honest to God.* London, 1963; on this, see E. Schillebeeckx, *Personale Begegnung mit Gott. Antwort an Robinson.* Mainz, 1963; idem, *Neues Glaubenverständnis. Honest to Robinson.* Mainz, 1964.
Schlier, H. "Kerygma und Sophia," in *Die Zeit der Kirche* (Freiburg, ²1958), pp. 206-32.
Schubert, K. *Der historische Jesus und der Christus unseres Glaubens.* Vienna, 1962.
Vorgrimler, H. (ed.). *Dogmatic vs. Biblical Theology.* Helicon, 1965.
Weber, G. *Religionsunterricht als Verkündigung.* Braunschweig, 1961; in connection with this, see J. Goldbrunner, "Unterricht oder Verkündigung," in *Katechetische Blätter* 88 (1963), pp. 59-63.

PART III

DO-C DOCUMENTATION
CONCILIUM

J. Britto Chethimattan, C.M.I./*Bangalore, India*

The Scope and Conditions of a Hindu-Christian Dialogue

O
n May 18, 1964, Pope Paul VI announced the establishment of a Vatican Secretariat for Non-Christian Religions. This was expected for about a year, during which time the desirability of such a Secretariat had been pointed out by several responsible persons. This Secretariat comes as a sequel to the Secretariat for Christian Unity established by Pope John XXIII in 1960 for contacts with non-Catholic Christian communities. The latter Secretariat has within a short period yielded abundant fruits of goodwill and mutual understanding between Christian communities that have been living far apart from each other with no appreciable contacts for centuries.

This good example given by the Secretariat, headed by the now world-famous Cardinal Bea, has raised sanguine hopes in all quarters concerning the new Secretariat. Several prominent Hindu scholars such as Sri K. M. Munshi have publicly expressed their appreciation of the move and showed willingness to enter

* J. BRITTO CHETHIMATTAN, C.M.I.: Born July 7, 1922 at Thottakad in Kerala, South India. He became a Carmelite of Mary Immaculate, studied philosophy and theology at the Gregorian University in Rome and was ordained in 1951. He is professor of dogmatic theology and prefect of studies at Dharmaram College in Bangalore, member of the editorial board of *Kathiroly* (a Malayalam theological quarterly) and *Indian Ecclesiastical Studies,* and associate editor of the Malayalam Catholic daily, *The Deepika.* His published works include several books in Malayalam, and a number of theological and popular articles.

into a religious dialogue with Christianity. For they all keenly feel the awkwardness of division and opposition between religions in a world painfully divided on several other issues. The one unifying principle in a divided world is the belief in a supreme reality, the source and author of all things.

I

VARIOUS ATTITUDES AND APPROACHES

Still, there lurks in several minds some ambiguity concerning the scope of such a Secretariat for dialogue. Several Hindu scholars, while evincing great enthusiasm for the proposed dialogue, have also expressed their doubts about the prospects of such a dialogue: The Catholic Church presents a dogmatic religion. It has its tenets of faith clear and definite, and even the pope or the General Council cannot change them. Then what is the point in entering into dialogue with other religions if Catholicism is so inflexible in its position? Some even expressed frankly the suspicion that the highly organized Catholic Church is opening an efficient Secretariat for facing the non-Christian religions in order to attract and absorb into its fold the followers of other religions.

Christian Approach to Hinduism

But the gradual development in the Christian attitude to Hinduism will show the proper scope of the new Secretariat. Since the advent of the Europeans in India early in the 16th century there have been sporadic and individual attempts to understand Hinduism, but real Christian interest in Hinduism is of recent origin. Only after the publication of several texts of Hindu scriptures in European languages, especially by scholars like Max Müller, Tibaut and others, did considerable widespread interest in Hinduism appear. Recently, some books on Buddhism and Hinduism have reached the popularity of best-sellers in the bookshops of London and Paris.

Humanist Approach

But all Christian scholars do not make the same kind of approach to Hinduism. There is first of all the humanist approach to Asiatic religions. The great orientalists in general belong to this category. They are in the classical tradition of seeking human nature across space and time. Their intention is to enlarge human consciousness and to integrate space and time in a broad and comprehensive humanism. They often confuse the idea of religion with that of civilization.

See, for example, how Sylvain Levi expresses his idea about the meaning of Asiatic religions:

"Life remains a point between two infinites of ignorance; but intelligence has gained ground on these two infinites. The human species, which it prolongs and which will prolong it, gives to man a first reason for existence which resolves nothing in the order of the transcendent, but which satisfies in some measure the demands of the most rigorous logic and reasoning. Man does not take the place of God; but humanity constructs a sort of bridge between him and God which hides the horror of the abyss gaping at both ends".[1]

Since such scholars are interested only in the human element of religion, they constantly try to sift out the common human factor of religions: Man at all times thinks, feels and loves in the same way. For some of them religion is just the "progressive formation of God". They interpret this progress either in a Hegelian way as the dialectical onward march of the human idea, or in the positivist style ascribing reality only to the law of progress of the successive individual realizations.

Attitude of Neutrality

Closely related to this is the attitude of neutrality of which Count Keyserling is a representative, as shown in his book, *The Travel Diary of a Philosopher*. In each country, by a sort of

[1] *L'Inde et Monde* (1925), pp. 132-3, cited by H. de Lubac, *La Rencontre du Bouddhisme et de l'Occident* (Paris, 1952), p. 264.

empathy he takes up the defense of the religion of the place: "Every appearance within its limits can give expression to Atman. . . . Every form of consciousness reveals a different layer of nature. He who dwells in the world of the Hindu is subject to influences and has experiences unknown to others". But back in America he is critical of all the Asiatic religions: ". . . the behaviour in practice of the average man in the East leaves more to be desired than that of the same class in the West. On the whole, we act better than we are".[2]

Among those who look at Hinduism as a religion, there are some who question the very possibility of an encounter between Hinduism and Christianity. Thus, Alan W. Watts pleads in *The Supreme Identity* that no attempt should be made to make a synthesis between Christianity and Hinduism: "A theology dealing with dogmatic, historical and sacramental ideas is an approach to reality utterly distinct from a 'metaphysical mysticism'. The two kinds of language cannot be fixed without hopeless confusion".[3]

Some even go to the extent of condemning Hinduism as totally erroneous. According to Hendrik Kraemer, its pretense of Brahma realization, the "Aham Brahmasmi" repeats the original sin of humanity, namely, of pretending to be equal to God.[4]

Paul Claudel, the French poet and orientalist, styles the attempt to discover the absolute within one's own self as "the silence of the creature cut apart in its total refusal, the incestuous quiet of the soul brooding upon its essential distinction".[5] But such criticisms often miss their point. All religions are not religions in the same sense of the term. Besides, as W. E. Hocking remarks: "Most of our criticisms of a religion other than our own are invalid for the simple reason that it is one thing for those who live by it and another for those who do not".[6]

---

[2] *The Travel Diary*, p. 595.
[3] *The Supreme Identity*, p. 12.
[4] *Religion and the Christian Faith* (London, 1956), p. 335.
[5] *Connaissance de l'Est*, cited by H. de Lubac, *op. cit.*, p. 272.
[6] *Living Religions and a World Faith* (1940), p. 57.

Syncretist Attitude

But today the great majority of scholars assume a syncretist attitude, pretending to imitate the bee that sucks the honey from every flower rather than the mosquito that is everywhere after blood. But they easily gloss over the fundamental differences. Aldous Huxley's *The Perennial Philosophy* and W. T. Stace's *Time and Eternity* are well-known examples of this syncretism. The artificial and standardized form of religion that such scholars present as the cream of all religions plays a little among religions the role that Esperanto has among languages. It only serves to increase the confusion rather than to reduce it. No one with a living religious faith will be satisfied with such a phantom religion. According to W. T. Stace, all religious expressions are merely evocative symbols, fruit of the human imagination trying to conceive the inconceivable ultimate reality. He tries to reduce all the major religions to this preconceived pattern, and thus succeeds only in doing injustice to all of them.

Someone has called religious syncretism spiritual fornication. Though the term appears rather strong, still it aptly describes the incongruity of the approach. The syncretist is guilty of a promiscuity in that he takes from each religion what catches his fancy and avoids what is irksome and calls for sacrifice. Thus, Joseph Hackin was taken up with the artistic aspect of Indian religions, especially the infinite benevolence that one calls *maitri,* and equanimity of soul, and he thought that it was the whole of religion.[7] Friedrich Nietzsche found in the Buddhist Nirvana the total religious phenomenon without any Platonic idea beyond, deliverance without a redeemer. But in his ultimate position he reached the extreme opposite to that of Buddhism, namely, that of considering as the ultimate moral goal, the joyful acceptance of the cycle of births and deaths, the sacred gift of saying "yes" to the "eternal return". Some even make impossible combinations. Thus, Max Scheler tries to identify the "Libido" concept of Freud and the instinct for death of the Buddhist doctrine as expressions of the same "sacred wisdom gliding towards the

[7] H. de Lubac, *loc. cit.,* p. 272.

silent Nothing and Eternal Death".[8] To say the least, as Huston Smith remarks, "The advocates of the essential unity of man's religions must meet the charge of superficiality".[9]

Some have recourse to this syncretist view of the equality of all religions just to plead that there is no need for discussion or dialogue on religious problems: Since basically all religions are the same there is no need to worry about the details. But they do not apply this basic equality of all men and the unity of their outlooks to avoid problems in other fields, scientific, cultural, social and economic. The fact seems to be that they are not thoughtful enough to realize the actual basic differences that do exist among men in the religious field. As Sankarâcharya says, Brahma is an existent reality; nobody thinks it legitimate to entertain one's own opinion that a post is a man or something else; one has to acknowledge it as a post. Similarly, our religious ideas and obligations have to be according to the reality that is Brahma. Acharya himself says that one who chooses to remain with one's own whims on the matter will be like the blind man who in good faith catches hold of the tail of a bull, thinking that it is a walking stick.

The basic fact here is that religion is not merely a set of principles to be learned by heart, or practices to be observed, but rather a concrete existence. It is life, man's life at its deepest level. Hence, as W. E. Hocking says: "The price of existence must be paid. We shall not arrive at the world faith by omitting the particulars". The polemist and syncretist forget this fact. The polemist considers his own religion in concrete and every other religion in abstract and as if from the outside. Hence, for him his own religion is true and every other false, or his own is complete truth, while others have only fragments of truth, or are only moments in the spiritual development already transcended. The syncretist, on the other hand, assumes arbitrarily that no religion is absolutely true and starts with the supposition that all religions are equally true and equally false. But to form a bal-

[8] *Ibid.*, cf. pp. 268-9; 275-6.
[9] *The Religions of Man*, p. 320.

anced judgment, each religion should be examined in concrete
from the point of view of its followers, from what it means for
their spiritual life. For as A. N. Whitehead says:

"Religion is the vision of something which stands beyond, behind, and within the passing flux of immediate things; something
which is real, and yet waiting to be realized; something which
is a remote possibility and yet the greatest of present facts; something which gives meaning to all that passes, and yet eludes ap-
prehension; something whose possession is the final good, and
yet is beyond all reach; something which is the ultimate ideal
and the hopeless quest".[10] In a sense it is God himself, the goal
of human aspirations.

In an encounter of persons who are equally interested in the
quest of this one absolute, a purely theoretical approach has
several disadvantages:

1. In theory each one may feel convinced of the truth of his
own position and any compromise on truth will be infidelity to
a sacred trust. Hence, in a theoretical discussion, each of the
parties comes with a sense of superiority that is apt to alienate
all sympathy of the opposite side.

2. The polemic and apologetic exigencies often drive one to
the extreme of thinking that there is no true or good point on
the opposite side. This will, by itself, defeat the very aim of the
encounter.

3. More than all these, a speculative approach reduces religion to a theory to be taken out of life and fought over with
abstract distinctions. It makes religion a set of principles and
conclusions, laws and observances. But fundamentally religion
is life. Indeed, definiteness of doctrine and certainty of tenets is
the essential requisite of any intelligent religious life. But doc-
trines of life should not be allowed to evaporate into abstract
ideas and juridical subtleties. Hence, the cold and indifferent
attitude of the scholar of comparative religion is the most ill-
suited in an encounter of religions.

[10] *Science and the Modern World*, c. 12.

The Dialogical Approach

Hence, the encounter that the new Secretariat is constituted to promote is the dialogical one of the meeting between persons and persons. In such an encounter of persons who sincerely live the truths of their own religion and honestly seek after the supreme, there is no room for superiority and inferiority attitudes. All are children of the same God, wayfarers on the same path. In such an encounter what is more important is a personal realization of the basic truths of religion in concrete life rather than a systematic and abstract knowledge of those truths. In this outlook, a theologian with a thorough knowledge of the truths of religion and a penetrating sense of analysis may be far inferior to a layman who has a deeper personal realization of some of those fundamental truths. Hence, in a religious dialogue individuals meet together in a spirit of humility and mutual respect. Not that objective truth is unimportant. No fruitful dialogue on religion can be had with a compromise on truth. But truth is no one person's monopoly. It is a free gift, the participation from the ultimate truth. Hence, one has to approach it with humility and with the conviction that one is unable to sound its depths perfectly.

II

PROSPECTS OF A HINDU-CHRISTIAN DIALOGUE

Basic Conditions for Dialogue

Prospects for a Hindu-Christian dialogue can be estimated only by examining how far the necessary conditions for any dialogue are actually verified. So that there may be a real and fruitful dialogue, the following conditions have to be satisfied:

1. In any dialogue the parties are supposed to meet each other on an equal footing, with an openness to truth. Dialogue is the meeting of two "Logoi" communicating with each other in the communion of their common understanding. Hence, if both or

either of the parties start with an absolute finality of their positions, there is no place for a dialogue. There should be openness
to truth from both sides. This does not mean that they should
be doubting the validity of their stands. Two can meet in dialogue even when they are absolutely sure of their positions, provided they have their minds open to the infinite truth that can
never be fully grasped by the human mind. A certain receptivity
from both sides is required. A sincere seeker of truth has to
widen the framework of his original authentic vision in a way
that will accommodate the elements of truth found anywhere and
everywhere. Truth does not contradict truth. Thus, to widen the
horizon of one's comprehension of all the newly discovered elements of truth is not an infidelity to truth, but part of that fidelity.
To refuse to do this is a sign of bigotry, which is infidelity to
truth.

Hence, the *sine qua non* condition of any dialogue is a humble mind that does not claim a monopoly on truth, but is deeply
conscious of the need for greater spiritual wealth and for widening the horizon of its spiritual vision.

2. The "communion" that is the basis of all dialogue demands
that we take for granted the sincerity and good faith of our partner. We have no other way to his interior except his words and
actions, and we have to accept the dictum, *nemo malus nisi
probetur*. Hence, a dialogue on religion should suppose that each
party takes its religion seriously and as a source of spiritual
nourishment. The history of every religion presents us with men
who have sincerely sought to do the will of God. "God is not an
acceptor of persons. All who sincerely seek him are acceptable
to him". This does not mean that all religions are equal, but only
that no religion is fully false. Each religion contains at least a
few basic truths, by which the spiritual life of its followers is
kept up and nourished. These basic intuitions are authentic and
should be preserved even in conversion.

3. Any dialogue to be fruitful should be conducted in an atmosphere in which the partners understand each other fully. For
this, a clarification of the basic positions and fundamental tenets

of both sides is quite necessary. The real point in a dialogue is in detecting where the parties really differ and in trying to resolve those differences. This clarification of basic positions may be done properly and easily through suitable publications written from an angle intelligible to the other side. In these, the whole religious position of the side concerned should be set forth without any preoccupation to hide inconvenient aspects. A sincere seeker of truth wants to face the whole truth even when it hurts.

4. Agreement in an intellectual encounter should be first on commonly realized rational truths. Hence, the right background for a religious dialogue is a common rational philosophy that is acceptable to both sides. For this, a sufficiently comprehensive system such as that of St. Thomas Aquinas or of Sankara should be taken and enlarged to include the discussion of all the main problems of philosophy.

In the light of these conditions, we may examine the prospects of a Hindu-Christian dialogue from the side of Christianity and from the side of Hinduism:

From the Side of Christianity

1. The willingness of the Catholic Church to meet other religions in dialogue is not merely a manifestation of her magnanimity, a concession made on her traditional stand of isolation and rigidity, although it may appear so against the background of her general policy of the past few centuries. But the dialogical attitude belongs to her very being and is an important note of her catholicity. Although her message is divine—the Good News of what Christ has accomplished in the name of humanity—still the message has to grow in a certain sense in width and depth with what she receives from every side. She will not be truly catholic unless she becomes incarnate in every land and culture and assumes all that can be assumed from their authentic religious past. Only in this way does she really go to every nation to preach the Gospel to every creature.

2. The very nature of her teaching mission demands a dia-

logical approach to cultures and religions. Of course, her mission is to preach and convert all to Christ. On the question of conversion, she can only repeat the answer St. Paul gave King Agrippa: "I would to God that, whether it be long or short, not only thou but also all who hear me today might become such as I am, except for these chains" (Acts 26, 29). But this is not sales promotion. A Christian does not preach merely for increasing the membership of his Church, community or party. His is a God-given mission, a command from the Lord to announce the divine message to every creature. St. Paul himself says: "For even if I preach the gospel, I have therein no ground for boasting, since I am under constraint. For woe to me if I do not preach the gospel! If I do this willingly, I have a reward. But if unwillingly, it is a stewardship that has been entrusted to me" (1 Cor. 9, 16-17). Sometimes Hindus accuse Christian missionaries of presumption, since they preach without themselves having fully realized what they preach. But the fact is that the Christian does not preach his own intuitions and experiences, but only the message that is in Christ's name and is contained in the death and resurrection of Christ.

Teaching itself implies a dialogue. A good teacher does not try to impose his ideas on the students. He knows that he cannot use such a method on a rational subject without turning him into some kind of automaton. True teaching is helping the student to learn, so that he may actively assimilate what is presented to him and make his own free judgment on the matter. This means a real dialogue between the teacher and the taught. Hence, the messenger of Christ can communicate his God-given message only in an atmosphere of healthy dialogue in which, not a selfish interest to win over the other to his own point of view, but the objective truth of the message stands out.

Similarly, when the Church invites all to be converted to Christ, she is not exerting pressure and presenting allurements to make them forget entirely their religious past and substitute something else in its place. This will introduce a break in the vital development of man and will be perversion rather than

conversion. Conversion, as the term itself suggests (*cum +
vergere*) is a turning back on oneself, a gathering of all one's
powers into one's authentic self. Hence, it is an invitation to
each one to be himself more fully than he is now, to break the
veil of self-satisfaction and cozy traditionalism and to discover
his own internal need for greater spiritual wealth in the light of
what Christ has said and done in history. Such an invitation can
be given only in a spirit of dialogue. Conversion is a continuous
process. Not only has the sinner to turn away from his evil ways
and become just, but also the just have to become more just, the
holy more holy. The preacher who exhorts to conversion has
himself need of conversion. Hence, it is only a mutual invitation
for emulation in inwardness, which can be made only in an atmosphere of dialogue.

3. That the dialogical aspect of Christianity was for a time
allowed to lie in obscurity was only an accident in history. From
the beginning, dialogue was the basic note of the Christian message. The Church appeared at the point of confluence of the
Egyptian, Babylonian, Greek and Semitic cultures and cults, and
it grew up by incorporating in its social structure whatever was
positive in these religious traditions. It appeared in Palestine as
the fulfillment of the expectations of Judaism, announcing the
long expected advent of the Messiah, emphasizing the new law
and the new kingdom. But it had to shift the emphasis to the
fundamental cosmic notions (of light and life, of the true sheep-
fold and of the living water, of the true gnostic community of
the illumined of God, and especially of the mystery of salvation)
before it could be taken to the Greek world by St. John and St.
Paul.

At the same time, the apostles, and even St. Paul, meticulously
followed in their personal observance the prescriptions of the
Jewish law, although they had to resist the imposition of the
ceremonies and rites of the law on the Gentile converts. St. Paul
readily recognized the divine testimony in the hearts of the Gentiles, who had no written law and preached to them the Unknown
God, whom they were already worshiping without knowing him.

He fights only against people like Elymas the magician (Acts 13, 8) and others who exploited the religious sentiment of the people for their own selfish motives. The books burned by the new converts at Ephesus, coming to the value of fifty thousand pieces of silver, were mostly magical books, distortions of religious beliefs (Acts 19, 19) and not genuine religious books.

We may summarize the whole Christian position in this matter in the words of Cardinal Newman: "The phenomenon, admitted on all hands is this: That great portions of what is generally received as Christian truth is, in its rudiments or in its separate parts, to be found in heathen philosophies and religions". Against those who argue, "These things are in heathenism, therefore they are not Christian", he answers: "We on the contrary prefer to say, 'These things are in Christianity, therefore they are not heathen'. That is, we prefer to say, and we think that Scripture bears us out in saying, that from the beginning the Moral Governor of the world has scattered the seeds of truth far and wide over its extent; that these have variously taken root, and grown up as in the wilderness, wild plants indeed but living". These represent the working of divine providence within the minds of individual persons and in the histories of particular races and nations.

The Church grew up by accepting and assimilating all these positive elements without losing her individuality and the integrity of her message. In this sense she is as old as the human race itself:

"She began in Chaldea, and then sojourned among the Canaanites, and went down into Egypt, and thence passed into Arabia, till she rested in her own land. Next she encountered the merchants of Tyre, and the wisdom of the East country, and the luxury of Sheba. Then she was carried away to Babylon, and wandered to the schools of Greece. And wherever she went, in trouble or in triumph, still she was a living spirit, the mind and voice of the Most High; 'sitting in the midst of the doctors, both hearing them and asking them questions'; claiming to herself what they said rightly, correcting their errors, supplying their defects, completing their beginnings, expanding their surmises, and thus gradually by means of them enlarging the range and refining the sense of her own teaching. So far then from her creed being of doubtful credit because it resembles foreign theologies, we even hold that one special way in which Providence has imparted divine knowledge to us has been by enabling her to draw and collect it together out of the world and in this sense as in others, to suck the milk of the gentiles and to suck the breast of kings." [11]

But in the encounter of the Church with Islam, Muhammadan political might posed a threat to Christian Europe, and unfortunately, force was resorted to in the support of religion. Similarly, in the missionary undertakings of colonial powers the military played a prominent part and the catholicity and spirit of dialogue of the Church was not very much in evidence. As a result, the work of evangelization also progressed at a slow pace. But this is only an accident in history owing to the interference of politics in religion, of Caesar in things of God. Hence, it is a constant danger that has to be avoided. The catholicity and dialogical spirit of the Church needs to be constantly reasserted lest one should seek shortcuts of expediency and opportunism in the furthering of the kingdom of God.

From the Side of Hinduism

In speaking about the prospects for a dialogue from the side of Hinduism we have to take into account the changes that have taken place in the Hindu mentality in recent times. These have created a climate of dialogue in religion:

1. Traditional Hinduism ascribed the pride of place to Advaita, beyond which and outside of which there is naught else to be learned, while this experience itself, being a personal realization, cannot be communicated to others. Hence, the Advaitic Guru remained in icy isolation with, at best, a smile of conde-

[11] Cardinal Newman, *Essays, Critical and Historical,* ii, p. 231.

scension and of distant compassion for the miserable disciple
bound by ignorance. He was merely a model or a sounding board
for concentrating the dissipated powers of the disciple. But today the fact is generally admitted and emphasized that such persons who have attained realization, the Jivanmuktas, are very
rare, if at all. If one asserts oneself as an Advaitin, that in itself
is a sure sign that he is not one: It is not known by those who
pretend to know it, while it is known by those who think that
they do not know, the Upanishad tells us. The so-called Advaitins
are only Advaitic dialecticians who have yet to strive for realization and have, hence, to be helped for it by others in various
ways. On the other hand, almost all the important writers of
modern Hinduism, especially Tagore, Aurobindo and Dr. S.
Radhakrishnan follow a *Viśiṣṭâdvaitic* trend of thought, in which
plurality has a meaning, and a permanent and eternal purpose.

2. National independence and the forces generated by it have
produced a change of outlook in Hinduism itself. The late Dr.
Devanandan summarizes these forces under four heads: (a) the
trend toward cultural unification; (b) the movement for a re-
patterning of society; (c) the urge for a reordering of the economic life of the people so that they benefit by modern technology; (d) and the prevailing quest for human solidarity.[12]

The sifting out of the cultural elements from strictly religious
beliefs and practices has served to narrow down differences between religious groups. The breakdown of the caste system and
other traditions has left the question of who is a Hindu rather
difficult to answer. In its wake, the Hindu missionary sometimes
takes up the advocacy of the equality of all religions. Technology,
which has emphasized the need for material progress and has
brought about a rational outlook on all matters, is a challenge
to religion to express the spiritual values of material goods, a
point left in obscurity by traditional Hinduism. Finally, the universal consciousness of human solidarity has brought poignantly
forward the incongruity of the religious divisions in humanity

[12] P. D. Devanandan, *Preparation for Dialogue* (Bangalore, 1964), pp.
56ff.

and has emphasized the need for a single religion for all humanity.

All these trends of modern thought have thrown a bright light on what was a blind spot in Hinduism, namely, the meaning of the world and of history, the proper place of the cultural and the cultual in approaching the absolute, and the importance of the social and universal character of man's religion—points that are uppermost in Christian consciousness. This change has facilitated a rapprochement between Hinduism and Christianity on present-day vital problems.

The Present Situation of the Dialogue

These thoughts on the need for dialogue on the part of both Christianity and Hinduism bring home to us the incongruity of the present situation, in which actually there is no dialogue but at best only two monologues. A necessary prerequisite for a fruitful dialogue is a clarification of the basic points of each side. Perhaps the greatest obstacle for a dialogue today is the lack of such clarification. From the Hindu side there are a good many publications that have set forth Hindu ideas in a way that is intelligible to the West. The works of Tagore, Aurobindo and Dr. S. Radhakrishnan and the publications of the Bharata Vidya Bhavan are generally available. Here one important drawback may be that the most vocal defenders of Hinduism are not its authentic representatives, but people who, thanks to a Western education, know more Western contemporary trends of thought than their own ancient tradition. Urged on by a propagandist enthusiasm, they easily fall prey to syncretism, relativism, and more often than not to religious indifferentism.

On the Christian side, too, the situation is not any better. In recent times we have several English publications on points of Christian doctrine available to the educated Hindu. But they are mostly published with the Western reading public in mind, and are, therefore, almost unintelligible to one brought up in the Indian tradition. Even those published in India are directed exclusively to Christian communities. Besides, they are mostly based on the technical theology manuals, which are almost entirely Western in outlook. It is doubtful if we can find a single authentic Christian treatise that may be placed in the hands of the Hindu, a book that speaks about Christianity in a language intelligible to him. The ordinary Hindu does not himself have the background for a proper understanding of the Bible. Spiritual books like the *Imitation of Christ* may do more harm than good. We cannot forget here the great service done by the so-called Calcutta School of Jesuits, Fathers Johanns, Dandoy and others. But their works are mostly comparative studies of Hinduism and Christianity, a stage that is already past. These books are of help more to the Christians than to the Hindus.

Hence, we have to rely on individual theologians to meet the Hindus in dialogue, which is rather an unreliable situation. Very few persons may be found among our Christian theologians and missionaries who are competent for such a delicate task. The Christian seminary training at present is conceived against a Western background, built upon the basis of Western philosophy. Hence, the priests who come out of these seminaries are not sufficiently conscious of the Hindu milieu in which they have to exercise their ministry, in spite of the increased emphasis placed on Indian topics in the seminary curriculum. Very few of them evince any real interest in meeting the Hindu in dialogue.

At present, the main source of inspiration for the dialogue is the missionary zeal of the Western missionaries who feel deeply their obligation to deliver the message of Christ to those Hindus forming the great majority in India. This is clear from the fact that in the several all-India conferences held so far on this problem—like the All-India Cultural Study Week held at Madras in December 1956, the Seminary Professors' Conference held at Bangalore in 1957 and the three Christian Colloquies on Hinduism held under the sponsorship of Dr. Cuttat—the great majority of participants were Europeans. These European missionaries who had their whole training in Europe, in spite of their great enthusiasm and burning zeal, find it an uphill job to get into the mentality of the Hindu thinkers. Hence, we Christians find ourselves in the preliminary stage of needing to expose Hinduism to Christians so that they may conceive their Christian message against a Hindu background.

III

THE DIALOGICAL ATTITUDE

Perhaps the first step toward a real dialogue should be to form the right mental attitude for it in the participants:

1. The first condition for a religious dialogue is to realize more deeply the positive values of one's own religious belief. The Hindu should purify his own conscience from all selfishness, blind traditionalism and everything else that may cloud his vision and fix his attention on the one absolute reality; he should see the supreme reality manifested in everything, and further try to understand the value of this world and of history and society in and through the supreme. In this way alone he can gain a real openness to the aspects of the supreme reality that the Christian message emphasizes. All closed rendezvous with one's own preconceived idea of the absolute forbids all discussion and slams the door on all dialogue.

The Christian, on the other hand, has to meet his Hindu brother in Christ. Christ is the fulfillment of all the intimate aspirations of man. In Christ alone all the multiplicity and variety of the creature can be attributed to the Godhead without in any way tainting the divinity: he is a single Person at home in two natures, the absolute and immutable divinity, and the perfect humanity. Hence, he is the one answer to the irreconcilable opposites of the transitory and limited world of beings and the supreme reality.

This deepening of religious faith is required as a precaution against two dangers usually occurring in religious encounter, namely, gnosticism and relativism. Gnosticism makes of religion a pure philosophy, a system of ideas to be speculated upon. One who is interested in merely comparing religions from the outside will miss the essential meaning of religion. Similarly, religious relativism, which considers each religion true for its own followers, denies the unity and universality of truth and is, therefore, infidelity to truth itself.

2. The second task in any dialogue is to enter as far as possible into the mind of the partner in dialogue and thereby widen one's horizon of religious vision. This means to place oneself in the point of view of the other side, as far as this can be done without compromising one's basic position. Thus, the Hindu should be ready to examine the claims of the historical Christ. According to the Christian point of view the reality of this world and the historic existence of Christ, the God-man, far from detracting from the absolute transcendence and infinity of God, actually demands it as the basis of their reality. Apparent contradictions may disappear on closer examination. Besides, the imperfections and limitations of the human understanding, especially in the present condition, also should be taken into account.

Similarly, the Christian should widen his horizon to include also the authentic dimensions of the Hindu experience. For this he does not need to bring into Hinduism elements that are entirely foreign to it. He should rather try to make explicit what is implicit in its authentic elements. In this way, he will be deepening Hindu experience itself. This is the task of the Christian missionary in every part of the world. Christ himself had to do it with regard to Judaism: "You search the Scriptures . . . And it is they that bear witness to me . . ." (John 5, 39). ". . . he interpreted to them in all the Scriptures the things referring to himself" (Luke 24, 27). But what the Old Testament contained about Christ was not a photograph of the future; what was only implicit in it had to be made explicit, and what was mere expectation had to be realized in concrete. St. Paul did the same to the Greeks. He preached to the Athenians the Unknown God to whom they had dedicated an altar. Clement of Alexandria found a great part of Christian doctrine implicit in Greek religious experience. Tertullian found everywhere the human soul naturally Christian. St. Gregory of Nyssa widened the Plotinian scheme of mysticism to include the whole of Christian experience. St. Augustine found in Neoplatonism almost everything of Christian faith except that the Word became flesh and died to redeem men:

"Thou didst provide me with certain books of the Platonists . . . And therein I read, not indeed in these words, but to the same purpose, enforced by many and divers reasons, that 'in the beginning was the Word, and the Word was with God, and the Word was God: the same was in the beginning with God: all things were made by him, and without him was nothing made: that which was made by him is life, and the life was the light of men, and the light shineth in the darkness, and the darkness comprehended it not'. . . . But, that 'he came unto his own, and his own received him not, but as many as received him, to them he gave the power to become the sons of God, even to them that believe on his name'. This I read not there.

"Again, I read there, that 'God the Word was born not of flesh nor of blood, nor of the will of man, nor of the will of the flesh, but of God'. But that 'the Word was made flesh, and dwelt among us', I read not there . . ." (*Confessions* Bk. vii, c. 9).

3. But even with all this widening of horizon there will be an area of real difference that cannot be glossed over. An important aim of the dialogue is to find out where the parties do really differ. These differences have to be squarely faced and their source patiently investigated. In this way we may be able to rise to a higher plane of thought where the apparent differences are adequately resolved and misconceptions corrected.

Thus, in Hinduism the absolute reality is unconditioned, sacred and impersonal, while in Christianity God is preeminently personal or rather tri-personal, most perfect and holy. Perhaps the reconciliation of the two views may be found in a deeper analysis of the notion of personality. In Hindu thought cosmogony is a mere manifestation of the divine, a mere symbol, while in the Christian view it is a creation out of nothing, a divine plan executed in the fullness of time. The synthesis between the two approaches may be found in the supernatural aspect of history, which draws all things toward the fullness of the divine good. Avatara for Hinduism is a periodic self-manifestation of God to restore and maintain the disturbed balance of right and wrong; while the Christian incarnation is the unique and unrepeatable event of the Word of God taking flesh at a particular moment of world history in order to restore everything to God in the unity of his own divine Person. There are several other points on which there is radical divergence between Christian and Hindu views. These differences should not be glossed over but should be squarely faced.

4. But this frank admission of sharp differences is not a reason why the two groups should live apart in camps at war with each other. Such differences are rather a challenge to the indomitable human will to work out a rapprochement without compromising truth. Hearts have to come together before intellects can settle their differences. Here we may take a lesson from the ecumenical movement in Christianity itself. It has revealed the serious and real differences that have kept the Christian communities apart for centuries; but by this realization hearts have only come closer with a grim determination that adequate solutions have to be discovered with light from the ultimate source of truth itself.

IV

A PRACTICAL SOLUTION

There is no doubt that radical differences between Hinduism and Christianity prevent a full religious participation between Hindus and Christians, especially in religious worship; they cannot be said to be members of the same family in the full sense of the term. Still, Hindus will admit the sincerity of Christians as seekers of truth, which is one and common to all. Christians on their part do not consider the Hindus away from the grace of God as long as they are in good faith and follow the dictates of their own conscience; they also, in the Christian view, are saved only through the grace of Christ, the one savior of the whole of humanity. Hence, there is every reason to express in everyday life this unity of all in the quest of the one absolute, and to seek to strengthen this union in every possible way:

1. One practical means will be for Hindus and Christians to meet in small groups in a spirit of prayer and meditation to listen to the voice of God within the cave of the heart. In this way, misunderstandings may be removed and positive religious understanding deepened. Only by this silent listening and prayerful discussion can we understand the Bible, which is the Word of God manifested through human history, and especially the Upanishads, which are the groanings of the human heart in intimate contact with the divine. St. Thomas Aquinas as the great Christian theologian learned more at the foot of the cross than from the big volumes he read, and Sankara as the great Acharya of Advaitins felt the need to pour forth his heart in his celebrated "Bhakti-stotrani".

2. Facing jointly the common problems on the social, cultural, economic and political fields is another concrete expression of the common religious concern. Most of these problems demand the concerted action of all who esteem the spiritual values of man. For, the onslaught of materialism and its various expressions are questioning basic human values almost in every field. In facing this common enemy of humanity itself, much can be done by the close cooperation of all who have the common bond of religion.

3. Finally, the vivid realization of the awkwardness of our religious divisions in an already divided world should bring home to us our inability to reach a solution by our own unaided efforts. This should persuade us to take refuge in prayer. Some of the prayers daily recited several times by Hindus emphasize our need for light and unity:

Gâyatri (Rg Veda III, 62, 10; cf. Brih. Up. V, 14, 1-6)

Om, Bhur, Bhuvanah suvah

Sat, Savitur varenyam
Bhargo devasya dhimahi
Dhiyo yo nah pracodayat!

Om, he fills the earth,
the atmosphere and heaven,
Let us meditate on that excellent
glory, of the divine Vivifier, Savi-
tuh. May he enlighten our understanding!

Introductory Prayer to some of the Upanishads:

Sahanâvavatu, saha nau bhunaktu,
saha vîryam karavâvhai, tejasvinâ-
vadhitamastu; mâvidviṣâvahai!

May (Brahman) protect us both;
May he enjoy us both; May we
work together; May the luminous
One be studied by us; May we
not hate each other!

The prayer taught us by Christ is equally universal in outlook
and comprehensive in its requests:

> Our Father who art in heaven,
>   hallowed be thy name.
> Thy kingdom come,
>   thy will be done
>   on earth, as it is in heaven.
> Give us this day our daily bread.
> And forgive us our debts, as
>   we also forgive our debtors.
> And lead us not into temptation,
>   but deliver us from evil.
>   (Matt. 6, 9-13)

PART IV

CHRONICLE OF THE
LIVING CHURCH

India and the Liturgy

P armananda Divarkar, S.J., wrote: "India has an 'anima naturaliter liturgica' (a soul that is liturgical by nature), inclined to worship God in symbol. The complaint of liturgists (and even of psychiatrists) in the West that one of their greatest difficulties is that people have lost the sense of symbol, that they do not see beyond the obvious reality and live confined in the present world, could not be made about us. Even the most sophisticated and Westernized of our citizens still respond to symbolism; they celebrate beautiful symbolic feasts and are attached to symbolic observances. We Christians, to whom so much of our native spiritual tradition is a closed book, have not altogether lost the sense of symbol. If it has not manifested itself in the liturgy, it is mainly because the liturgy has so far been closed to any cultural adaptation" ("Towards an Indian Liturgy", in *India and the Eucharist* [Eucharistic Congress of Bombay, Nov.-Dec., 1964]).

THE PROBLEM OF ADAPTATION

Father Parmananda continues with the observation that there have been valiant attempts at adaptation, mostly by foreigners and particularly in the past few decades. By and large their attempts have not been very successful, except perhaps in the field of religious music. He wonders whether this should not warn us against tampering with so sacred a thing as the liturgy, even though the Church now allows the introduction of native elements, provided they are worthy of acceptance. He does not think so. The chief reasons for past failures is, in his view, precisely that the liturgy could not be touched. For this meant that the movement lacked inspiration, without which there can be no true creativity but only ineffective imitation. Inspiration comes from a living experience, from vital contact with a significant reality. Moreover, the fruitful energy, the balance and judgment, required for effective action, depend on proper adjustment to environment and the so-called sense of belonging.

Now the wellspring of the Christian life is the eucharistic liturgy in which the mystery of salvation is enshrined; and the place where Christians belong most is around the eucharistic altar. If they are not entirely at home at the altar, if they cannot fully enter into the liturgy, their growth is stunted and they become in some measure unproductive. A movement of adaptation that excludes the liturgy is not only condemned to the sterile effort of adding a few decorative effects to what remains at bottom something strange and foreign, but also to failure even in this trivial task; it will lack inspiration, for it will be deprived of a living experience of the Christian mystery. Of course, there will still be vital contact with the mystery by virtue of sacramental grace, but this grace does not operate at the level of experience. This grace must come from a liturgy that is meaningful in all its dimensions.

According to Father Parmananda, Indians ought to realize the consequences of the fact that their Christian life has stood outside their native culture. They have become estranged from this culture even in what may be called the natural spheres of life: since culture is the natural means for self-expression and development, they have not even been fully human, let alone fully Christian. What creative effort can one expect in such a situation?

In the author's view, the chief drawback of their unadapted

liturgy does not lie in the fact that it is foreign, but that it represents a stage of development far in advance of their actual condition. He refers to his book, *The Church and the Nations* (Sheed and Ward), and to his article in *Jeunes Eglises* (n. 13, 1962), and explains the situation as follows:

"The Church came to us—that is, to most of our Christian communities in India—not as a tiny mustard seed that could grow into a mighty tree by feeding on the native soil, but as a formidably developed institution, rigidly organized on the post-Tridentine pattern, almost entirely prefabricated. There are many who think that it is an advantage that we have not had to go through tedious stages of development, that we are no different from any Church in Europe. But a living being cannot save time by dispensing with the process of growth; that can only lead to loss of vitality and ultimate infertility. The Church is a living being, and it is no advantage to us that we have not begun at the beginning and grown up normally. We do not even know what it is to grow, for we have known only one kind of Church, and a very rigid kind at that. We cannot imagine that the Church can change and still be the true Church, whereas the very opposite is true; she must change in order to be the true Church, a living body and not a petrified fossil."

These factors, according to this author, are the cause of the distressing but undeniable sterility of the Indian Church, despite the deep eucharistic piety of the Indian people, despite their fidelity and zeal. They have produced some passable imitations but created nothing—nothing even remotely comparable to the achievements of Western Christendom or, for that matter, to what has been achieved in their own country, outside the Church. And this in spite of their boast that their Christian heritage goes back to the apostles and to the greatest missionary of modern times. In a footnote Father Parmananda adds:

"It is not a pleasure to acknowledge this, and our efficient organization and many large institutions may be mentioned in refutation. But how many great personalities and works of genius can we list? How many significant movements have we launched?"

He asks whether there is now hope of evolving a liturgy that is fully Christian and truly Indian, that can appeal to the soul of modern India, and he is convinced that the answer is in the affirmative. The way toward this end cannot be traced in detail. It is attractive to speculate on the subject, but hardly profitable. There can be no preconceived solutions. They must be found as the situation develops—*solvitur ambulando*. And he concludes:

"India is a vast, multiform and rapidly changing country; but it is one country, and we are told that whilst the liturgy is now flexible, notable differences in adjacent regions must be avoided (Constitution on the Liturgy, Art. 23). We would suggest that there should be clearly recognizable degrees of flexibility within the same rite, so that some features, like the part of the president or celebrant, are allowed less diversity and evolution than others, such as what belongs to the people's participation. In this way some practical problems can be solved and a fine balance achieved between uniformity and permanence on the one hand, and satisfactory adaptation to varying needs on the other.

"The task ahead is enormous; but it is not impossible, and it is supremely worth the effort. Someday we shall reach the goal. Then the Bride of Christ will stand at the altar of Sacrifice resplendent in gold from Ophir. Ophir is believed to have been a port in western India, and the gold spoken of in the ancient prophecy is India's contribution to the varied beauty of the Church—and how great could be that contribution can be determined from the immense treasury of good things that the heavenly Father has created, sanctified, enlivened and bestowed on his children in India, through Christ our Lord! Through Him and with Him and in Him, is to the Father almighty, in the unity of the Holy Spirit, all honour and glory through endless ages. Amen."

THE CHRISTIAN-HINDU ENCOUNTER

In the same collection of essays much thought is given to the great cultural crisis which India experiences today as a result of increasing industrialization, and to its place among the nations of the world. The study of this crisis is also most important for the encounter between Christianity and Hinduism in India. The image presented by the authors of this collection is far from one-sided. Already in the first essay, "Indian Spirituality and the Eucharist", Bede Griffiths asks: "What can India give in return to Christ?" He counters the question with other questions (the task, indeed, must still be begun). He writes:

"May we not believe that if the Christian mystery could be studied in the light of the Vedanta, it would throw a new light on it, even more profound than that which was shed by Greek philosophy, and give rise to a genuine Christian Vedanta? But still more, may we not believe that if the devotion of the Indian soul which has centred on Rama and Krishna and Siva for so many centuries, could find in Christ its object of worship, as the one Person, in whom the ineffable mystery of the Godhead—the Parabrahman—is contained, and who makes it present in the reality of a human nature, which calls forth the greatest love which man can know, we should see a flowering of Christian devotion, perhaps even greater than that of the Christian Middle Ages?"

Samuel Rayan, S.J., points to Acharaya Vinoba Bhave, who has been laboring since 1951 for voluntary land-reform in order to improve living conditions. But even if this is taken as more than a drop in the ocean, India as a whole still faces a very heavy task. The late Pandit Nehru described it in the following terms:

"The world today is going through mighty changes, revolutionary transformations. One cannot imagine what physical and biological upsets are coming, but an important thing to remember is that the extraordinary changes have made the necessity of social change more paramount than ever before." This means that we have to develop a new concept of man: "What the world is groping for today seems to be a new dimension in human existence, a new balance. Only a fully integrated man with spiritual depth and moral strength will be able to meet the challenges of modern times. Material advance without spiritual balance can become disastrous."

From the point of view of the Western mind, India's vision of man and his world is dominated by traditional Hinduism. In his essay on "The Eucharist and a New Personalism for India", the Indian Jesuit, Samuel Rayan, mentions "our many unsocial attitudes and anti-social acts, the maze of corruption on all levels and in every department of life, ruthless hoarding and exploitation of crises, adulteration of food and even of medicine, neglect of common property, shabby services". He relates all this to Hindu ethics, which indeed imposes social obligations on the individual but is primarily concerned with self-discipline in view of the liberation of the individual. In its relation to the absolute and to worship, Hinduism does not know such a thing as a "People of God"—its thought is individualistic. Here, too, Christianity can be a message of deliverance for India.

India's cultural crisis urgently requires a dialogue between the traditional Hindu outlook on history and the Christian theological interpretation of history. This is the theme of "The Eucharist and the Quest of India for a New Vision of History", by Sebastian Kappen, S.J. India's traditional view of history is based on the pattern of cosmic processes. The sun rises in the morning, sets at evening, only to rise again with the following dawn. Plants spring up from the womb of the earth, grow, and then decay, thus returning to where they came from, until they sprout once again from the soil. The seasons, too, follow a pattern of birth, death, and rebirth. The Indian mind has always thought of man as part of the cosmos, and therefore subject to the law of cyclic return. History is "a perpetual creation, perpetual preservation, perpetual destruction", as is written in the Vishnu Purana (I, 7). Man and the world are not created by the deity, but emanate from Brahman into which they are reabsorbed at the end of every *Kalpa* and where they remain in a stage of pure potency until they emanate again, thus initiating a new cycle.

This view does not invite man to consider himself and his

world, the past, present and future, as something important. Precisely because everything "emanates" from the deity and develops as a cosmic process, there is little sense of vocation, or mission that, insofar as "history" is concerned, is so typical of Israel and Christianity. In traditional India there is a cult and veneration of the past, with a tendency toward a certain nostalgia for the golden age that has gone by. The Indians of today, however, begin to see this rightly as an immature attitude that they are growing out of. The repetitive pattern of world cycles leaves no room for a future that has an appeal. The values of the present are not carried over into the future since they are doomed to destruction in an eventual *pralaya*. All that man creates, therefore, is stamped with the sign of death. The new creation that follows the night of Brahman is not any the richer for the achievements of the past. Further, since the end of each world period is nothing more than a mere return to the beginning, nothing new, nothing original, ever happens in history. The conviction that history has no definitive end, together with the idea of the transmigration of souls, deprives life on earth of its unique character, and overemphasizes the "vanity" of all human activity. Yet, underneath, there lives a profound longing for escape from the ever-turning cycle of *samsara*. Otherwise, how is it that Indians have never been able to reconcile themselves to this cyclic view of history? This hope of escape, however, is exclusively a matter of the individual; the community as such is condemned to the everlasting misery of repeated existences.

The message of Christianity, culminating in the eucharist, can free India from this oppressive cyclic view of history and give it a new "humanism", a new image of man and his world, which it so badly needs in its present cultural crisis. India, in its turn, can remind the Western Christian of the fact that he is but a pilgrim on this earth, that the whole creation lies in travail, that the shape of this world passes. It is to be hoped that the Eucharistic Congress of Bombay has stimulated the dialogue between India and Christianity toward further progress.